THE BARBOUR
BIBLE
ATLAS

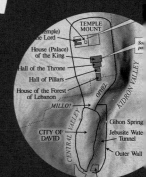

CHRISTOPHER D. HUDSON
GENERAL EDITOR

DAVID BARRETT
CARTOGRAPHER

TODD BOLEN
PHOTOGRAPHER

BARBOUR
PUBLISHING

Satellite terrain imagery produced with data provided by the Global Land Cover Facility, http://www.landcover.org. Author: MDA Federal 2004. Landsat GeoCover 2000/ETM+ Edition Mosaics. Sioux Falls, South Dakota: USGS.

All elevation data was created from data supplied by Shuttle Radar Topography Mission (SRTM), a project of the National Aeronautics and Space Administration (NASA). A full description of this data can be found at http://www.usgs.gov.

Photo and illustration credits:
All maps created by David Barrett (www.BibleMapper.com).
All photos taken from the library of Todd Bolen (www.BiblePlaces.com).
Special acknowledgement is made for the following images:
Page 28: Library of Congress, Prints & Photographs Division, LC-DIG-matpc-06959.
Page 92: British Museum © Copyright the Trustees of the British Museum.
Page 110: British Museum © Copyright the Trustees of the British Museum.
Page 126: Istanbul Archaeological Museum, Istanbul.

Published by Barbour Publishing, Inc., 1810 Barbour Drive, Uhrichsville, Ohio 44683, www.barbourbooks.com

Our mission is to inspire the world with the life-changing message of the Bible.

Member of the
Evangelical Christian
Publishers Association

Printed in China.

CONTENTS

DEDICATION

To Caleb, Ryan, and Analiese.
The Bible is the most important book in the world. I hope books
like this one help you understand it a little bit better.

INTRODUCTION

When Moses, Ezra, or Luke wrote books that later became part of the Bible, they had no way of envisioning readers living in the twenty-first century. As they wrote, they probably had their own children, grandchildren, and even great-grandchildren in mind—people they knew would understand the regional and geographical references in their writings.

For Bible readers today, however, thousands of years have passed, and those references have become obscure. And beyond the years, thousands of miles now separate most readers from the original locations of these stories, so we are not able to envision the landscapes and geography involved. When the Bible refers to the mountains of Israel, for example, we probably envision what we expect the mountains to look like. When we read about the countryside where Jesus preached, we may picture fields similar to those located near our homes.

Most of the time, those preconceived images aren't accurate. When David hid from Saul at En Gedi, he wasn't hiding in a charming, comfortable cave. When Jonathan ambushed the Philistines, he didn't sneak up quietly on a grassy, gentle trail. And when the people rallied for war, they prepared to fight their enemies over difficult and rocky terrain—scenes difficult to imagine for modern readers who only know highly technological warfare.

This book can change the way you read the Bible. The photos in this book, which were taken exclusively from the collection of Todd Bolen, help give readers a more accurate picture of the colors, landscapes, and terrain of Bible lands. The maps, created by brilliant cartographer David Barrett, help today's reader understand what it was like for Jesus, Joshua, and the people of Israel to crisscross a country about the size of New Jersey—usually by foot.

To help your Bible reading and study, we've arranged these pages so they follow the order of the Bible's books. By arranging the maps and images this way, we hope this book can provide some of the context and insight the original readers of the Bible would have had.

Christopher D. Hudson
General Editor

INTRODUCTORY MAPS

THE HOLY LAND TODAY

Modern-day Israel became a state after Britain withdrew from Palestine in 1948. The United Nations voted to establish two states in the region: one Jewish, one Arab. While Israel accepted the plan and declared her independence, the local Arabs and other regional nations rejected the proposal.

Since its foundation in this modern era, the small Jewish state has fought a series of wars against Arab neighbors—finally signing a peace treaty with Egypt in 1979 and Jordan in 1994. Today, significant conflict remains with the Palestinians (who live primarily in the West Bank and Gaza Strip). With few natural resources, Israel has built its economy on technology, tourism, and national defense. The population living in Israel numbers over nine million.

Israel is one of the few countries in the region whose citizens participate in a democratic electoral process, a free economy, and freedom of the press.

The holiest place in Israel is the Temple Mount, which remains under Muslim control. It holds religious significance for Jewish, Christian, and Muslim worshipers alike. The photo shows a Jewish man praying at the "Western Wall." This portion of the wall is a sacred part of the compound wall of the Jewish temple that the Romans destroyed in AD 70. Millions of people of all faiths (mostly Jewish) have prayed at this site, often sliding slips of paper containing prayers between the rocks of the wall.

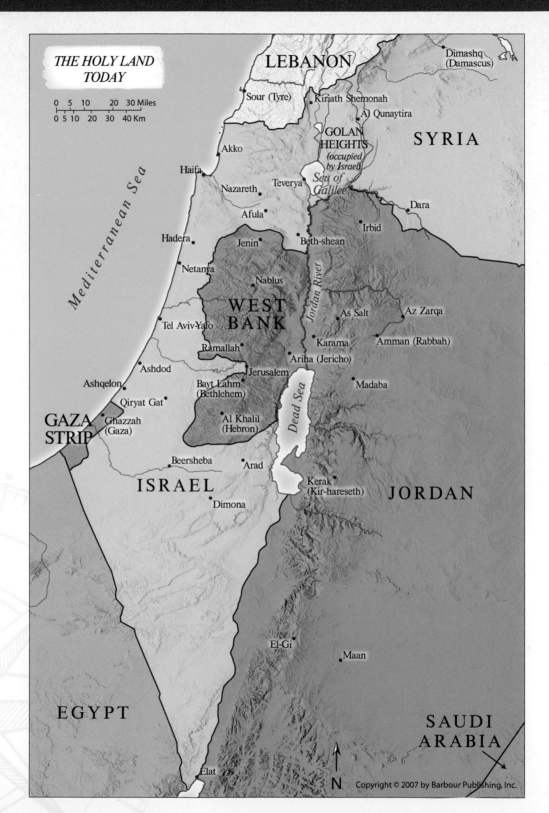

THE HOLY LAND TODAY

0 5 10   20   30 Miles
0 5 10 20   30   40 Km

LEBANON

Dimashq
(Damascus)

Sour (Tyre)

Kiriath Shemonah

Al Qunaytira

GOLAN
HEIGHTS
*(occupied
by Israel)*

SYRIA

Akko

Haifa

Mediterranean Sea

Nazareth

Teverya

*Sea of
Galilee*

Dara

Afula

Irbid

Hadera

Jenin

Beth-shean

Netanya

Nablus

Jordan River

As Salt

Az Zarqa

WEST
BANK

Tel Aviv-Yafo

Ramallah

Karama

Amman (Rabbah)

Ashdod

Ariha (Jericho)

Jerusalem

Ashqelon

Bayt Lahm
(Bethlehem)

Madaba

Qiryat Gat

GAZA
STRIP

Ghazzah
(Gaza)

Al Khalil
(Hebron)

Dead Sea

Beersheba

Arad

ISRAEL

Kerak
(Kir-hareseth)

JORDAN

Dimona

EGYPT

El-Gi

Maan

SAUDI
ARABIA

N

Elat

Copyright © 2007 by Barbour Publishing, Inc.

9

GEOGRAPHY OF THE HOLY LAND

The climate of Israel varies greatly depending on the time of year and the location. Areas in southern Israel, such as the Negev, are very dry—receiving less than ten inches of rain each year (see photo at bottom). Vegetation in this area is sparse, being mostly populated with wild desert scrub and occasional acacia trees, which spot the landscape (see photo on page 26).

In the northern region, rain is much more plentiful—especially during the months of December through February—which makes the landscape significantly more lush than in the south (see photo below). Snowfall is rare but does occur in the Golan Heights region.

The varied climate and landscape became a backdrop used by biblical writers. Below are two examples:

The Lush Northern Region:

For the LORD your God is bringing you into a good land—a land with streams and pools of water, with springs flowing in the valleys and hills; a land with wheat and barley, vines and fig trees, pomegranates, olive oil and honey; a land where bread will not be scarce and you will lack nothing; a land where the rocks are iron and you can dig copper out of the hills (Deuteronomy 8:7–9).

Judean Desert:

O God, you are my God, earnestly I seek you; my soul thirsts for you, my body longs for you, in a dry and weary land where there is no water (Psalm 63:1).

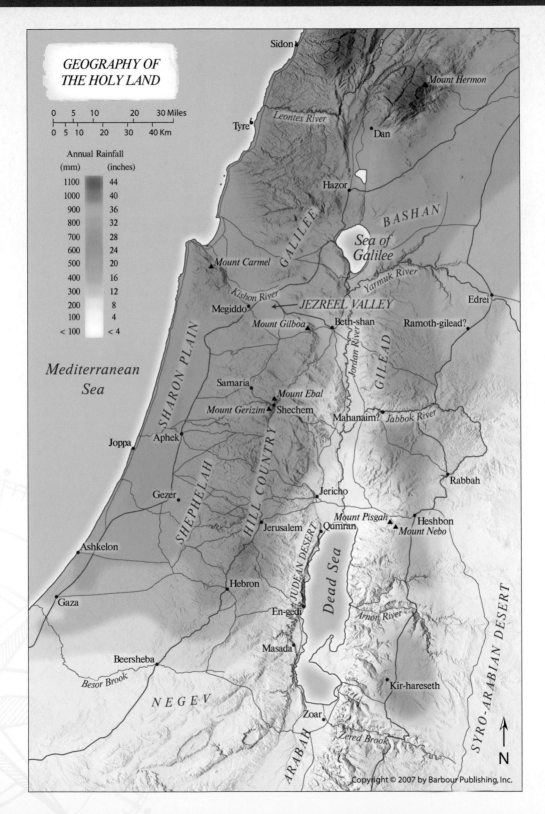

GEOGRAPHY OF THE HOLY LAND

0 5 10   20   30 Miles
0 5 10   20   30   40 Km

Annual Rainfall
(mm)   (inches)
1100   44
1000   40
900   36
800   32
700   28
600   24
500   20
400   16
300   12
200   8
100   4
< 100   < 4

Sidon

Mount Hermon

Leontes River

Tyre

Dan

Hazor

BASHAN

GALILEE

Sea of Galilee

Mount Carmel

Kishon River

Yarmuk River

Megiddo

JEZREEL VALLEY

Edrei

Mount Gilboa

Beth-shan

Ramoth-gilead?

Mediterranean Sea

Samaria

Mount Ebal

GILEAD

Jordan River

Mount Gerizim

Shechem

Mahanaim?

Jabbok River

SHARON PLAIN

Joppa

Aphek

Rabbah

Gezer

SHEPHELAH

HILL COUNTRY

Jericho

Ashkelon

Mount Pisgah

Heshbon

Jerusalem

Qumran

Mount Nebo

JUDEAN DESERT

Dead Sea

Hebron

SYRO-ARABIAN DESERT

Gaza

En-gedi

Arnon River

Masada

Kir-hareseth

Beersheba

Besor Brook

N E G E V

Zoar

Zered Brook

ARABAH

↑
N

Copyright © 2007 by Barbour Publishing, Inc.

11

THE LANDS OF THE BIBLE TODAY

Though only the approximate size of New Jersey, the land of Israel is filled with people of many religions and cultures.

Founded as a Jewish homeland, the country of Israel's population today consists of both those who identify themselves as Jewish (75%) and those who practice Islam (17.5%). The remaining residents practice Christianity, Baha'i, Druze, and other world religions. And while many identify themselves as "Jewish," most do so because of their Hebrew descent not because of their strict religious practices.

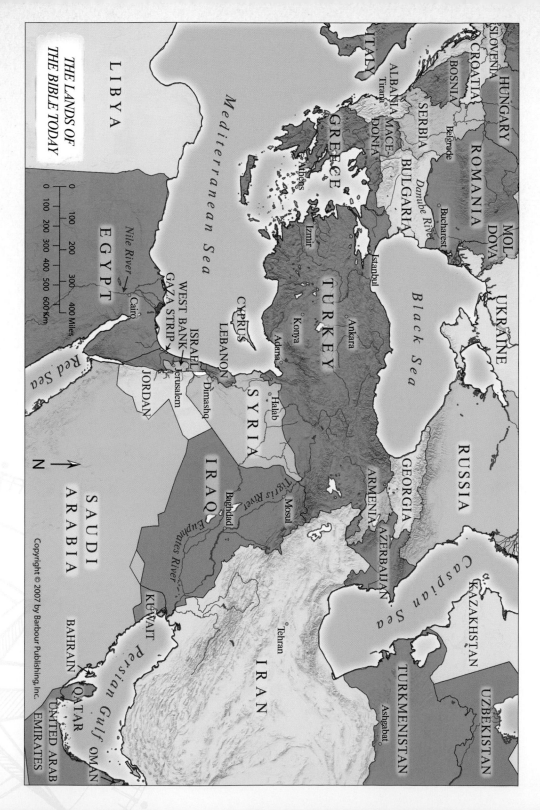

THE LANDS OF
THE BIBLE TODAY

LIBYA

EGYPT

Nile River

Cairo

Mediterranean Sea

Red Sea

N

SAUDI
ARABIA

KUWAIT

BAHRAIN

QATAR

UNITED ARAB
EMIRATES

OMAN

Persian Gulf

IRAN

Tehran

IRAQ

Baghdad

Mosul

Tigris River

Euphrates River

JORDAN

ISRAEL
Jerusalem

WEST BANK
GAZA STRIP

LEBANON

Dimashq

SYRIA

Halab

CYPRUS

Adana

Konya

TURKEY

Ankara

Izmir

Istanbul

Athens

GREECE

ITALY

ALBANIA
Tirane

MACE
DONIA

BOSNIA

CROATIA

SLOVENIA

HUNGARY

SERBIA

Belgrade

BULGARIA

Danube River

ROMANIA

Bucharest

MOL
DOVA

UKRAINE

Black Sea

GEORGIA

ARMENIA

AZERBAIJAN

RUSSIA

Caspian Sea

KAZAKHSTAN

TURKMENISTAN

Ashgabat

UZBEKISTAN

0
100
200
300
400 Miles

0
100
200
300
400
500
600 Km

Copyright © 2007 by Barbour Publishing, Inc.

13

THE PENTATEUCH

Mediterranean Sea

Hazor

Megiddo

Beth-sh

ISRAEL

Jerusalem

Jericho

Gaza   Hebron

MOA

Beersheba   **JUDAH**

xandria

Sin (Pelusium)

LOWER   Zoan

Migdol

EDOM

Rameses   Tahpanhes

EGYPT   Pithom?

Pi-beseth (Bubastis)

GOSHEN   Way to Shur

Brook of Egypt?

On (Heliopolis)

SINAI

Great Pyramids

Ezion-geber?   Elath

Memphis (Noph)

PENINSULA

MIDIAN

(claimed by Egypt)

Oxyrhynchus

Rephidim?

▲

Mount Sinai? (J. Musa)

Nile River

Red Sea

Abydos

NATIONS OF THE ANCIENT WORLD

The Bible's account of the global flood reports the story of Noah and the world-wide devastation he witnessed. With everyone else dead, Noah and his family were the only people left to repopulate the earth. Thus, every person on earth is descended from the three sons of Noah: Ham, Shem, and Japheth. The map on the next page captures the likely location of each people group and their probable patriarch.

The time line below highlights some of the biblical history that occurred between Noah and the time of the Hebrew kings.

2165 BC	Abraham is born.
2070 BC	Sodom and Gomorrah are destroyed.
1922 BC	Jacob marries both Rachel and Leah.
1805 BC	Joseph dies.
1700 BC	The life of Job? (Exact timing is unknown.)
1526 BC	Moses is born.
1450 BC	God speaks to Moses from the burning bush.
1400 BC	The time of the Judges begins.
1050 BC	Saul becomes the first king of Israel.

The biblical timeline continues on page 96.

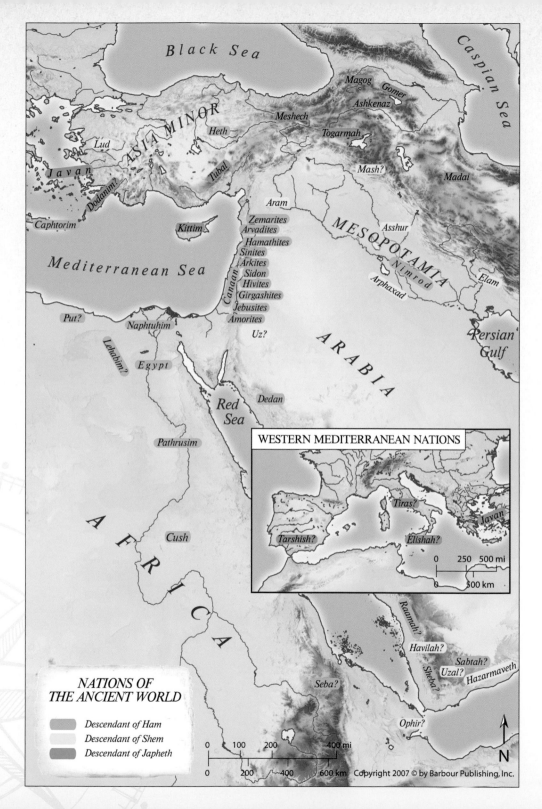

Black Sea

Caspian Sea

Magog
Gomer
Ashkenaz
Meshech
ASIA MINOR
Heth
Togarmah
Lud
Mash?
Javan
Tubal
Madai
Dodanim?
Caphtorim
Kittim
Aram
MESOPOTAMIA
Asshur
Mediterranean Sea
Zemarites
Arvadites
Hamathites
Nimrod
Sinites
Elam
Arkites
Canaan
Sidon
Arphaxad
Hivites
Girgashites
Jebusites
Amorites
Put?
Naphtuhim
Uz?
ARABIA
Persian
Gulf
Lehabim?
Egypt

Red
Sea
Dedan

Pathrusim

WESTERN MEDITERRANEAN NATIONS

Tiras?
Javan
Tarshish?
Elishah?

0   250   500 mi
0   300 km

AFRICA

Cush

Raamah?

Havilah?
Sabtah?
Uzal?
Sheba?
Hazarmaveth

Seba?

NATIONS OF
THE ANCIENT WORLD

Ophir?

N

Descendant of Ham
Descendant of Shem
Descendant of Japheth

0   100   200   400 mi
0   200   400   600 km   Copyright 2007 © by Barbour Publishing, Inc.

NEAR EAST DURING THE TIME OF THE PATRIARCHS

The story of God's people begins with Abram (later known as Abraham) in the land of Ur. While Abram was living in the region known as Babylonia, God appeared to him and instructed him to travel to Canaan—known today as Israel. This thousand-mile journey became a major turning point in human history.

The story of Abraham (Genesis 12–25) includes God's promise of a son whose descendants would populate the promised land. During Abraham's lifetime, he lived in Canaan, moved to Egypt, and returned to Canaan.

Throughout the centuries, Abraham has been a key figure in the Jewish, Christian, and Islamic religions. His central place in the faith of many has caused Abraham's traditional burial site (located in Hebron) to be seen as one of the most holy places in the Middle East (see photo). This location is believed to be the burial place of Abraham, Sarah, Isaac, Rebekah, Jacob, and Leah. The building which now houses this location was built by Herod the Great.

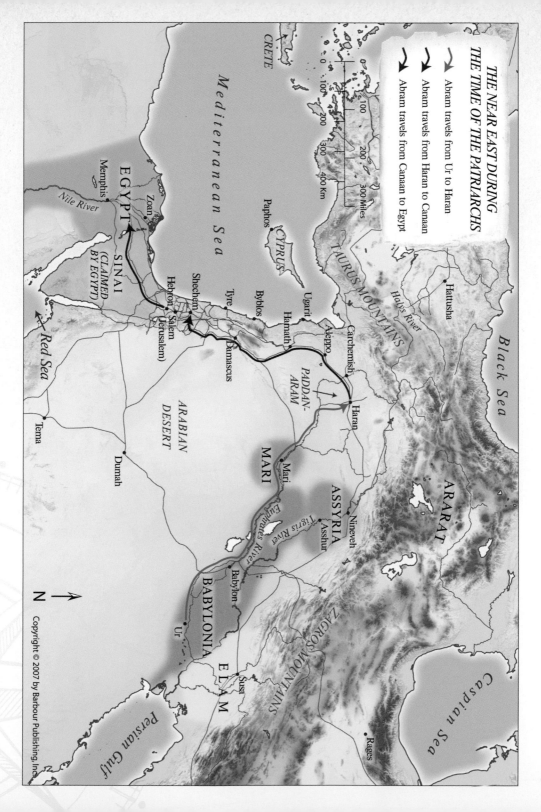

THE NEAR EAST DURING
THE TIME OF THE PATRIARCHS

Abram travels from Ur to Haran

Abram travels from Haran to Canaan

Abram travels from Canaan to Egypt

Mediterranean Sea

CRETE

CYPRUS

Paphos

Byblos

Tyre

Ugarit

Hamath

Aleppo

Carchemish

Hattusha

TAURUS MOUNTAINS

Halys River

Black Sea

PADDAN-
ARAM

Haran

Damascus

Shechem

Salem
(Jerusalem)

Hebron

EGYPT

Zoan

Memphis

Nile River

SINAI
(CLAIMED
BY EGYPT)

Red Sea

Tema

Dumah

ARABIAN
DESERT

MARI

Mari

Euphrates River

Tigris River

ASSYRIA

Asshur

Nineveh

ARARAT

ZAGROS MOUNTAINS

Babylon

BABYLONIA

Ur

ELAM

Susa

Rages

Persian Gulf

Caspian Sea

N

0   100   200   300   400 Km

0   100   200   300 Miles

Copyright © 2007 by Barbour Publishing, Inc.

CANAAN DURING THE TIME OF THE PATRIARCHS

Abraham's nephew, Lot, lived near the cities of Sodom and Gomorrah. When a coalition of four kings conquered the cities, they carried off Lot and his family as captives of war (see Genesis 14). When Abraham heard that Lot had been taken captive,

Abraham mobilized his own militia, pursued the kings, and won Lot's freedom.

As nomads, Abraham and his sons built their wealth through large flocks. The photo contains a scene of herds in the land of Beersheba, similar to the herds that would have grazed during the time of Abraham and his descendants.

Two generations after Abraham, Jacob and Esau became rivals for their father Isaac's blessing and wealth. In order to receive the blessing that Isaac planned to give to Esau, Jacob deceived his father. This enraged Esau, and caused Jacob to flee his home and seek refuge with his uncle Laban for twenty years before returning to Canaan. Esau pursued Jacob—but their meeting ended with reconciliation (see Genesis 32–33).

Throughout the stories of the patriarchs, common themes include faith, prayer, and worship. Frequently, the patriarchs made stops along their journeys to build altars to God. The map to the right records the locations of many of these altars.

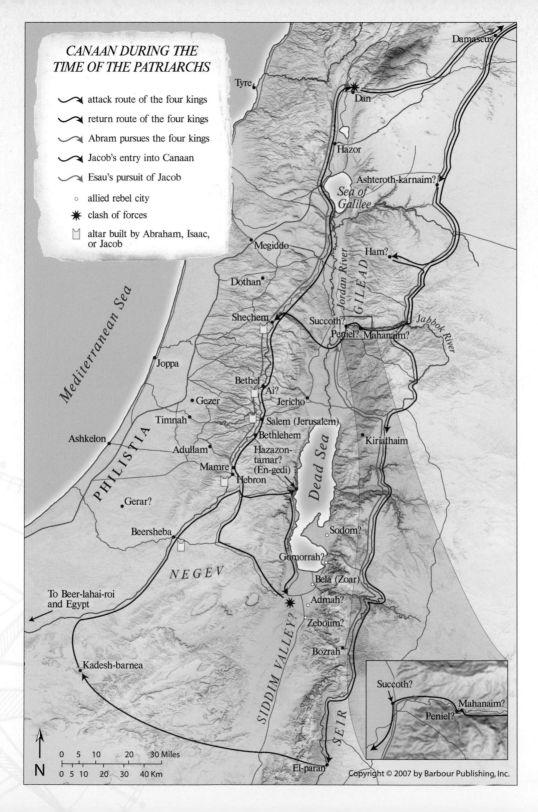

CANAAN DURING THE TIME OF THE PATRIARCHS

- ∿ attack route of the four kings
- ∿ return route of the four kings
- ∿ Abram pursues the four kings
- ∿ Jacob's entry into Canaan
- ∿ Esau's pursuit of Jacob
- ○ allied rebel city
- ✳ clash of forces
- ⌂ altar built by Abraham, Isaac, or Jacob

Damascus

Tyre

Dan

Hazor

Ashteroth-karnaim?

Sea of Galilee

Megiddo

Ham?

Dothan

GILEAD

Jordan River

Shechem

Succoth?

Peniel? Mahanaim?

Jabbok River

Mediterranean Sea

Joppa

Bethel

Ai?

Jericho

Gezer

Salem (Jerusalem)

Timnah

Bethlehem

Ashkelon

Adullam

Hazazon-tamar? (En-gedi)

Kiriathaim

PHILISTIA

Mamre

Dead Sea

Hebron

Gerar?

Beersheba

Sodom?

NEGEV

Gomorrah?

Bela (Zoar)

To Beer-lahai-roi and Egypt

Admah?

Zeboiim?

Bozrah?

SIDDIM VALLEY?

Kadesh-barnea

SEIR

N

0 5 10   20   30 Miles
0 5 10   20   30   40 Km

El-paran

Copyright © 2007 by Barbour Publishing, Inc.

Succoth?

Mahanaim?

Peniel?

21

EGYPT IN THE BIBLE

Located to the southwest of the promised land, Egypt frequently enters into the biblical narrative as the setting for key stories. Below are some of the many occurrences of Egypt in the Bible:

- Genesis 12: Abram moves to Egypt to escape a famine in the land.
- Genesis 37: Joseph is sold into Egyptian slavery.
- Genesis 47: Jacob and his sons move to the land of Goshen, where their descendants live for four hundred years—eventually becoming slaves of the Egyptians.
- Exodus 13–19: Moses leads the people out of Egyptian slavery to Mount Sinai (see page 24).
- 1 Kings 3: King Solomon makes an alliance with Egypt.
- 1 Kings 11: Jeroboam lives in Egyptian exile until the death of King Solomon.
- 2 Kings 23 and 2 Chronicles 35: King Neco of Egypt battles Josiah (see page 92).
- 2 Chronicles 12: King Shishak of Egypt attacks Jerusalem.
- Matthew 2: Mary, Joseph, and Jesus flee to Egypt.
- Acts 8: The Ethiopian eunuch travels through Egypt on his way back to Ethiopia (see page 148).

Historians agree that the great pyramids of Egypt (see photo) were built about one thousand years before the Israelite people initially moved to Goshen (see Genesis 47). While the pyramids are never mentioned in the Bible, the view of the impressive buildings may have been shared by many of the biblical characters who sojourned in Egypt.

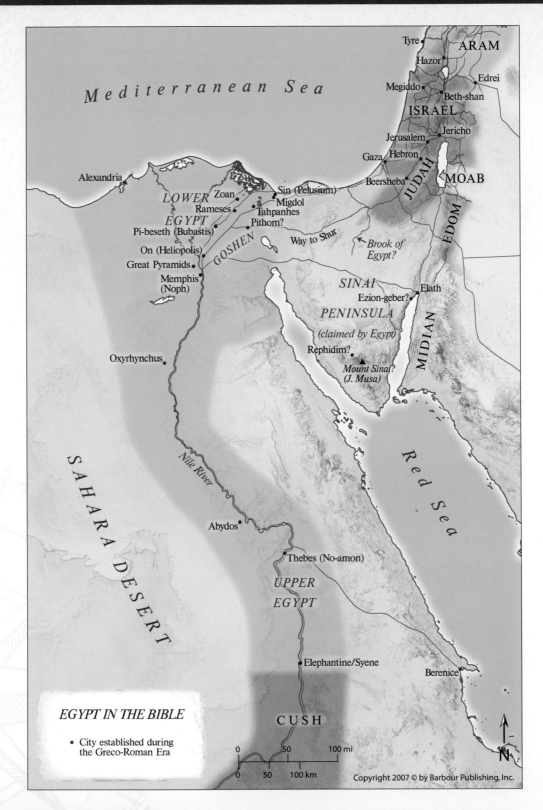

Mediterranean Sea

ARAM

Tyre
Hazor
Edrei
Megiddo
Beth-shan
ISRAEL
Jerusalem
Jericho
Gaza
Hebron
Beersheba
JUDAH
MOAB
EDOM

Alexandria

LOWER
EGYPT
Zoan
Sin (Pelusium)
Rameses
Migdol
Tahpanhes
Pithom?
Pi-beseth (Bubastis)
Way to Shur
Brook of
Egypt?
On (Heliopolis)
GOSHEN
Great Pyramids
SINAI
Memphis
(Noph)
PENINSULA
Ezion-geber?
Elath
(claimed by Egypt)
MIDIAN
Rephidim?
Oxyrhynchus
Mount Sinai?
(J. Musa)

Red Sea

Nile River

SAHARA DESERT

Abydos

Thebes (No-amon)

UPPER
EGYPT

Elephantine/Syene
Berenice

CUSH

EGYPT IN THE BIBLE

• City established during
the Greco-Roman Era

0   50   100 mi

0   50   100 km

N

Copyright 2007 © by Barbour Publishing, Inc.

23

THE EXODUS FROM EGYPT

While Sunday school teachers refer to the Red Sea as the location of Moses' great confrontation with Pharaoh's army, the Hebrew language found within the book of Exodus is less precise. Because most of the Israelite people were enslaved in the region of Goshen, the location of the event may have been the actual Red Sea or one of the lakes to the north.

After God miraculously delivered the Israelites from the pursuing Egyptians, Moses led the people south to Mount Sinai, which most likely was located in the southern end of the Sinai Peninsula. It was at Mount Sinai that the people received instructions from God that included the Ten Commandments (see Exodus 20).

While Michelangelo's Moses (see photo) depicts a young man, Moses took leadership of the people of Israel when he was eighty years old. He had spent the previous forty years living as a nomadic shepherd in dry, arid regions. It's likely that during these decades in the wilderness, Moses grew in his faith and learned practical lessons about living in barren climates. This skill would prove useful as he led the people out of the fertile region of Goshen into the dry wilderness they would end up inhabiting for forty years.

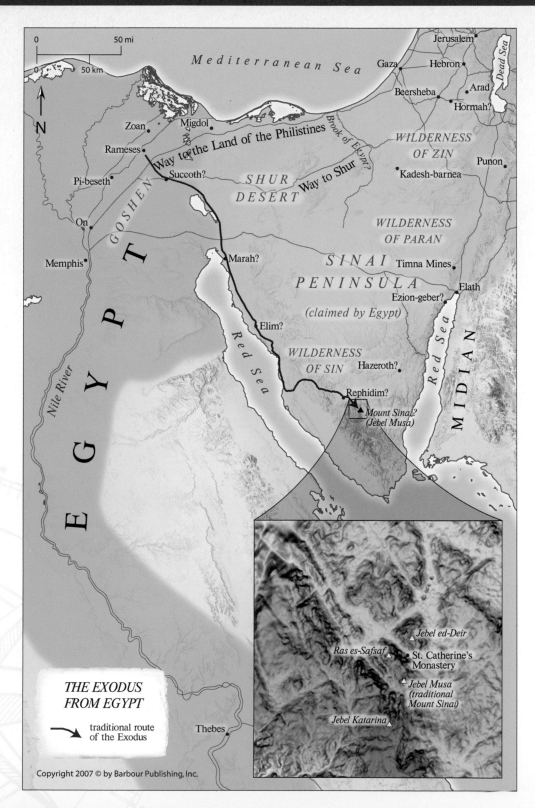

THE EXODUS
FROM EGYPT

traditional route
of the Exodus

Copyright 2007 © by Barbour Publishing, Inc.

EVENTS IN THE WILDERNESS

The Israelites' route through the Wilderness of Sin was through dry, uneven landscapes that were occasionally spotted with acacia trees. The dense wood of these trees yielded a durable product that the Israelites used to build the tabernacle and its accessories (see Exodus 25–27).

This photograph was taken in the southern Sinai Peninsula, where most scholars believe the Wilderness of Sin was located. (This area was named for a regional deity, not because of a sinful act.) The difficult and arid terrain makes it understandable why the Israelites often complained about their constant lack of food and water. Here in this wilderness, God began to provide daily manna for the people to eat (Exodus 16).

While the people camped at Kadesh-barnea, Moses sent twelve spies into the promised land through a southern route (Numbers 13), and the resulting story is well-known: Ten spies said that the enemies were too powerful to defeat, while two spies (Joshua and Caleb) pressed the people to trust God for victory. After the people sided with the ten spies, God pronounced His severe judgment (Numbers 14). In an effort to skirt God's discipline, a contingent of men armed themselves in a rash effort to conquer the promised land. Against Moses' advice, these Israelite soldiers marched north and were soundly defeated by the Amalekites and Canaanites (Numbers 14:40–45).

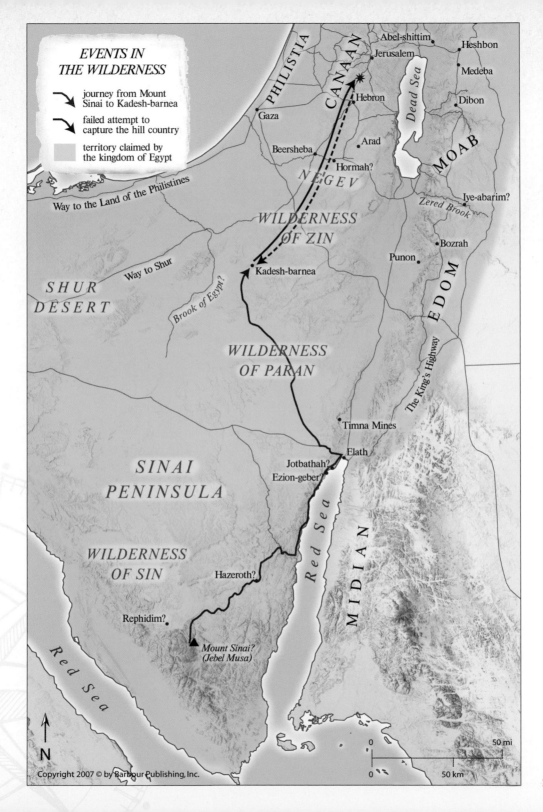

EVENTS IN
THE WILDERNESS

→ journey from Mount
Sinai to Kadesh-barnea

⇢ failed attempt to
capture the hill country

territory claimed by
the kingdom of Egypt

PHILISTIA

CANAAN

Abel-shittim

Jerusalem

Heshbon

Medeba

Hebron

Dead Sea

Dibon

Gaza

MOAB

Beersheba

Arad

Way to the Land of the Philistines

Hormah?

NEGEV

Iye-abarim?

Zered Brook

WILDERNESS
OF ZIN

Way to Shur

Bozrah

SHUR
DESERT

Brook of Egypt?

Kadesh-barnea

Punon

EDOM

WILDERNESS
OF PARAN

The King's Highway

Timna Mines

SINAI
PENINSULA

Elath

Jotbathah?

Ezion-geber?

Red Sea

MIDIAN

WILDERNESS
OF SIN

Hazeroth?

Rephidim?

Mount Sinai?
(Jebel Musa)

Red Sea

0   50 mi

N

0   50 km

Copyright 2007 © by Barbour Publishing, Inc.

27

JOURNEY TO THE PROMISED LAND

Because of the Israelites' rebellion, God condemned them to live in the wilderness for forty years. During this time, every living adult (with the exception of Joshua and Caleb) died because of their disobedience to God. Joshua, Caleb, and the children (who would grow into adults during this time) would be the only ones to enter the promised land (Numbers 14).

Toward the end of their journey, the Israelites requested permission from King Sihon of the Amorites to peacefully pass through his territory. Not only did he refuse, he also mobilized his army and attacked God's people. The Israelites soundly defeated the Amorites, as well as King Og of Bashan (Numbers 21).

The people finally arrived at Abel-shittim and received God's instructions for taking the land. This was the final leg of their journey with Moses as their leader. Before Moses died, however, God directed him to climb Mount Nebo. From this height of 3,300 feet, Moses received a clear view of the promised land (see photo showing this same view). Moses died on top of the mountain and was buried by God Himself in a secret grave (Deuteronomy 34). Joshua assumed leadership of the people and led the conquest of Canaan.

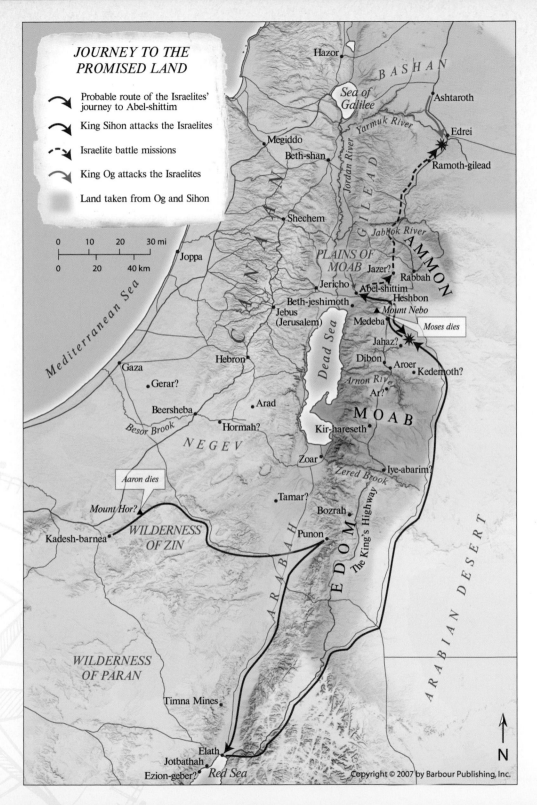

JOURNEY TO THE
PROMISED LAND

Probable route of the Israelites'
journey to Abel-shittim

King Sihon attacks the Israelites

Israelite battle missions

King Og attacks the Israelites

Land taken from Og and Sihon

0   10   20   30 mi

0   20   40 km

Hazor

BASHAN

Sea of
Galilee

Ashtaroth

Edrei

Megiddo

Beth-shan

Ramoth-gilead

GILEAD

Jordan River

Yarmuk River

Jabbok River

AMMON

Shechem

PLAINS OF
MOAB

Jazer?

Rabbah

Jericho

Abel-shittim

Heshbon

Beth-jeshimoth

Mount Nebo

Moses dies

Jebus
(Jerusalem)

Medeba

Joppa

Mediterranean Sea

CANAAN

Dead Sea

Jahaz?

Dibon

Aroer

Kedemoth?

Hebron

Arnon River

Ar?

Gaza

M O A B

Gerar?

Arad

Beersheba

Hormah?

Kir-hareseth

Besor Brook

N E G E V

Zoar

Zered Brook

Iye-abarim?

Aaron dies

Tamar?

Bozrah

Mount Hor?

Punon

WILDERNESS
OF ZIN

Kadesh-barnea

ARABAH

E D O M

The King's Highway

A R A B I A N   D E S E R T

WILDERNESS
OF PARAN

Timna Mines

N

Elath

Jotbathah

Ezion-geber?   Red Sea

Copyright © 2007 by Barbour Publishing, Inc.

29

BALAAM BLESSES ISRAEL

After hearing about the Israelites' swift military successes, the people of Moab grew fearful of their new, powerful neighbors. Rather than pursue direct military action, King Balak of Moab sought divine help.

Balak sent emissaries from Moab and neighboring Midian to recruit a well-known soothsayer named Balaam. After receiving visions from God, Balaam agreed to travel to Moab and meet with the king.

While on their way to Moab, Balaam's donkey began to act strangely. The beast refused to stay on the path and even crushed Balaam's foot against a wall. In anger and frustration, Balaam beat the animal, which responded by talking in a human voice.

Upon hearing the voice, Balaam's eyes were opened—and he saw that God's angel was blocking the path. The donkey had actually saved Balaam's life. With a new respect for the power of God, Balaam continued on the southern journey to Moab.

Balak received Balaam and together they hiked along some taller mountains so that the king and soothsayer could view the Israelites firsthand.

Balaam, following specific instructions from the one true God, refused to curse the people but blessed them instead. Read the intriguing story of Balaam and his talking donkey in Numbers 22–24.

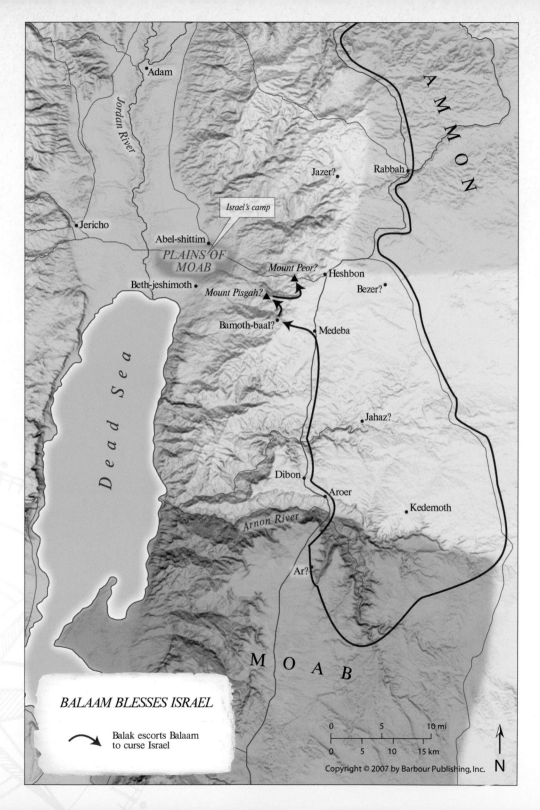

Adam

Jordan River

Jazer?

Rabbah

A
M
M
O
N

Israel's camp

Jericho

Abel-shittim

*PLAINS OF
MOAB*

Mount Peor?

Heshbon

Bezer?

Beth-jeshimoth

Mount Pisgah?

Bamoth-baal?

Medeba

D e a d   S e a

Jahaz?

Dibon

Aroer

Kedemoth

Arnon River

Ar?

M   O   A   B

BALAAM BLESSES ISRAEL

Balak escorts Balaam
to curse Israel

| 0 | | 5 | | 10 mi |
| 0 | 5 | 10 | 15 km | |

Copyright © 2007 by Barbour Publishing, Inc.

N

BOUNDARIES OF THE PROMISED LAND

The southern section of the Dead Sea (also known as the Salt Sea) pictured here became a natural boundary between the people of Israel and the people of Moab. God carefully described the extent of Israel's promised land using features such as the Dead Sea, the Jordan River, and the Mediterranean Sea (see the details recorded in Numbers 34).

As the people approached the promised land, the tribes of Manasseh, Gad, and Reuben realized that the plains on the eastern side of the Jordan River would be very suitable for their large herds. While not originally part of the boundaries promised by God, Moses agreed that they could acquire this eastern land as their own (Numbers 32).

The map to the right shows that the land that was ultimately occupied by the Israelites under Joshua's leadership was only a portion of the land that God had originally promised them in Numbers 34. Rather than being an act of disobedience, this more likely demonstrated that the people knew they didn't have the population or resources to settle the entire promised area. They lived with smaller boundaries, trusting God to fulfill His promises of Exodus 23:29–30, "But I will not drive [your enemies] out in a single year, because the land would become desolate and the wild animals too numerous for you. Little by little I will drive them out before you, until you have increased enough to take possession of the land."

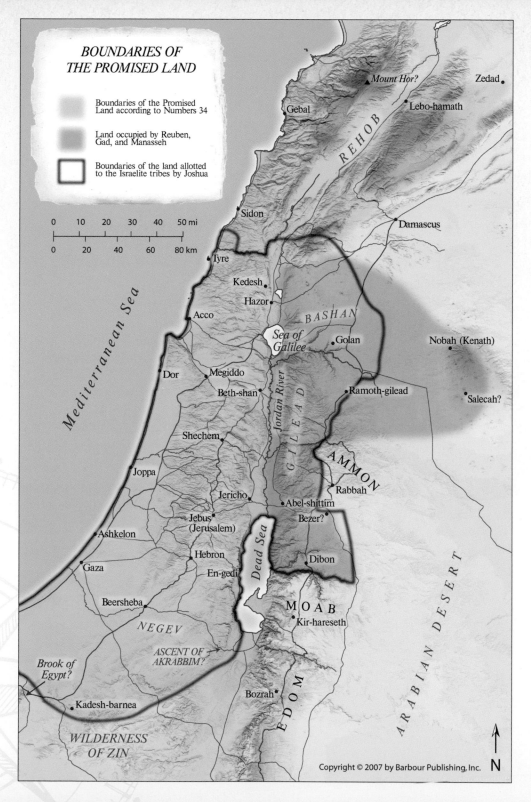

BOUNDARIES OF
THE PROMISED LAND

Boundaries of the Promised
Land according to Numbers 34

Land occupied by Reuben,
Gad, and Manasseh

Boundaries of the land allotted
to the Israelite tribes by Joshua

0   10   20   30   40   50 mi

0   20   40   60   80 km

Mount Hor?

Zedad •

Gebal •

REHOB

Lebo-hamath •

Sidon •

Damascus •

Tyre •

Kedesh •

Hazor •

BASHAN

Acco •

*Sea of
Galilee*

Golan •

Nobah (Kenath) •

Mediterranean Sea

Dor •

Megiddo •

Jordan River

Ramoth-gilead •

Salecah? •

Beth-shan •

G I L E A D

Shechem •

A M M O N

Joppa •

Rabbah •

Jericho •

Abel-shittim •

Jebus
(Jerusalem) •

Bezer? •

Ashkelon •

Dead Sea

Hebron •

Dibon •

Gaza •

En-gedi •

Beersheba •

M O A B

Kir-hareseth •

NEGEV

A R A B I A N   D E S E R T

*ASCENT OF
AKRABBIM?*

*Brook of
Egypt?*

Bozrah •

E D O M

Kadesh-barnea •

*WILDERNESS
OF ZIN*

Copyright © 2007 by Barbour Publishing, Inc.

N

33

HISTORICAL AND POETICAL BOOKS

ISRAEL ENTERS THE PROMISED LAND

While action-minded readers enjoy reading about the conquests of Jericho and Ai (Joshua 6–8), the stories of Israel's spiritual stops during the journey are equally important.

After miraculously crossing the Jordan, the people of God immediately worshiped God by building an altar (Joshua 3–4).

After defeating Jericho and Ai, the people paused again to worship God. Following the instructions given by Moses (Deuteronomy 11:29 and Deuteronomy 27), one half of the people stood at Mt. Gerizim and one half stood at Mount Ebal and shouted specific blessings and curses according to Moses' instructions. With the people assembled, Joshua read the Law of Moses in its entirety to the people (Joshua 8:34–35).

God did not haphazardly select the site of this worship service. The historic city of Shechem lies between these mountains, and it was the first place in Canaan that Abraham built an altar after being promised that his descendants would inherit this land (Genesis 12:6–7).

Abraham's grandson Jacob settled at Shechem and built an altar after being reunited with Esau (Genesis 33:18–20). Additionally, Jacob's twelve sons lived here while grazing their flocks (Genesis 37:12–13). By worshiping in this place, the people celebrated that they had finally come home.

The photo on this page is a view of Mt. Ebal taken from Mt. Gerizim.

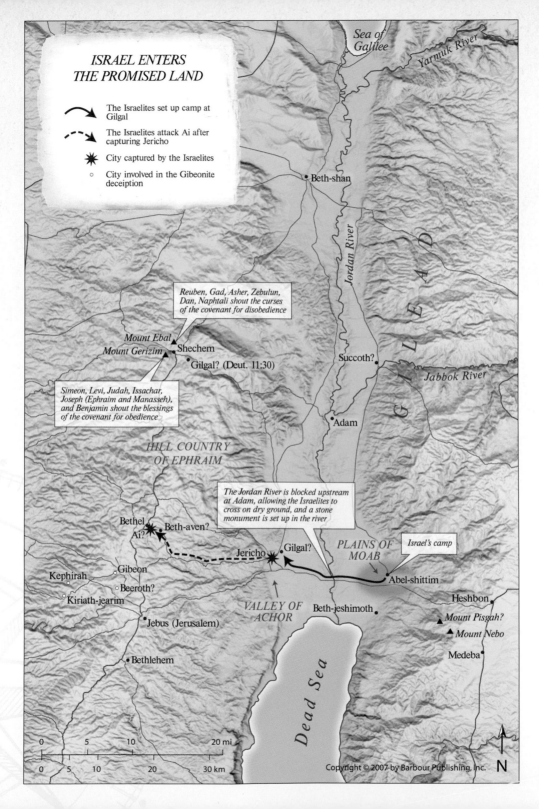

ISRAEL ENTERS THE PROMISED LAND

↷ The Israelites set up camp at Gilgal

⇢ The Israelites attack Ai after capturing Jericho

✸ City captured by the Israelites

○ City involved in the Gibeonite deception

Sea of Galilee

Yarmuk River

Beth-shan

Jordan River

G I L E A D

Succoth?

Jabbok River

Reuben, Gad, Asher, Zebulun, Dan, Naphtali shout the curses of the covenant for disobedience

Mount Ebal
Mount Gerizim Shechem
Gilgal? (Deut. 11:30)

Adam

Simeon, Levi, Judah, Issachar, Joseph (Ephraim and Manasseh), and Benjamin shout the blessings of the covenant for obedience

HILL COUNTRY OF EPHRAIM

The Jordan River is blocked upstream at Adam, allowing the Israelites to cross on dry ground, and a stone monument is set up in the river

Bethel Beth-aven?
Ai?

Jericho Gilgal?

PLAINS OF MOAB

Israel's camp

Abel-shittim

Kephirah Gibeon
Beeroth?
Kiriath-jearim

VALLEY OF ACHOR

Beth-jeshimoth

Heshbon

Mount Pisgah?
Mount Nebo

Jebus (Jerusalem)

Medeba

Bethlehem

Dead Sea

0   5   10   20 mi

0   5   10   20   30 km

Copyright © 2007 by Barbour Publishing, Inc.

N

ISRAEL'S BATTLES FOR THE PROMISED LAND

The Bible records supernatural events that occurred as Israel conquered Jericho. Recent archaeological discoveries corroborate biblical events. Findings include:

- At the time the city fell, Jericho's mud brick walls unexpectedly collapsed in some areas (Joshua 6:20).
- Jericho's buildings were destroyed by fire (Joshua 6:24).
- The discovery of many storage jars filled with grain. This substantiates the biblical account that the battle took place after the spring harvest (Joshua 3:15) and that the people did not plunder the city (Joshua 6:18).
- A portion of the wall did not collapse. This is consistent with the belief that Rahab's house may have been part of the wall (Joshua 6:22). See photo.
- The city remained vacant for generations after this victory (Joshua 6:26).

Soon after these victories, the Gibeonites tricked the Israelites into making an alliance (Joshua 9). God used that alliance to provide a decisive battle against five Amorite kings (see the green lines). Once they defeated these kings, the Israelite army moved through the region and conquered the southern portion of the country (Joshua 10). Joshua and the armies regrouped in the city of Gilgal (Joshua 10:43).

After seeing their southern neighbors defeated, the Canaanite people in the north (represented by the blue lines) joined forces in a futile attempt to oppose the Israelites (Joshua 11). Joshua moved his armies from Gilgal and defeated these kings as well. An extensive catalogue of military victories can be found in Joshua 12.

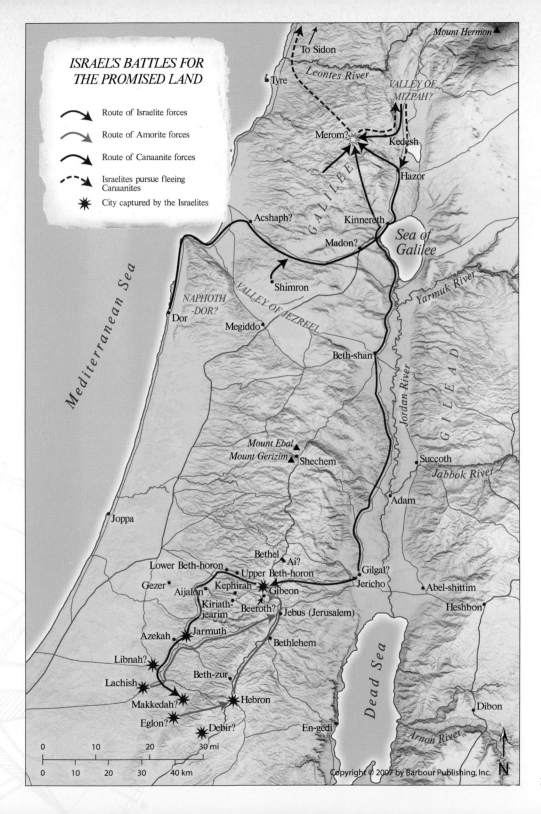

ISRAEL'S BATTLES FOR
THE PROMISED LAND

Route of Israelite forces
Route of Amorite forces
Route of Canaanite forces
Israelites pursue fleeing
Canaanites
City captured by the Israelites

Mount Hermon

To Sidon

Tyre

Leontes River

VALLEY OF
MIZPAH?

Merom?   Kedesh

Hazor

G A L I L E E

Acshaph?   Kinnereth

Madon?   Sea of
Galilee

Shimron

Yarmuk River

Dor

NAPHOTH
-DOR?

VALLEY OF JEZREEL

Megiddo

Beth-shan

Mediterranean Sea

G I L E A D

Jordan River

Mount Ebal
Mount Gerizim   Shechem   Succoth
Jabbok River

Adam

Joppa

Bethel
Lower Beth-horon   Ai?
Upper Beth-horon   Gilgal?
Gezer   Kephirah   Jericho   Abel-shittim
Aijalon   Gibeon
Kiriath-   Heshbon
jearim   Beeroth?
Azekah   Jebus (Jerusalem)
Jarmuth
Libnah?   Bethlehem
Beth-zur
Lachish   Dead
Makkedah?   Hebron   Sea
Eglon?   Debir?
En-gedi   Dibon

Arnon River

0   10   20   30 mi

0   10   20   30   40 km

Copyright © 2007 by Barbour Publishing, Inc.

N

39

THE TRIBAL ALLOTMENTS OF ISRAEL

Joshua 13–19 records the allotment of land granted to each tribe of Israel. The priestly tribe of Levi, however, did not receive a specific region as an inheritance. Rather, they received forty-eight cities scattered throughout the other tribal allotments—perhaps to make their spiritual influence felt throughout the whole nation (Joshua 21).

Joshua 20 records that six cities were designated as cities of refuge (indicated in white). In order to ensure that anyone needing to flee to one of these cities could arrive safely within a day or two, the cities were strategically located throughout the country. These specially designated cities reflect the high value placed on human life in ancient Israelite society. Life was so sacred that if someone was killed—even accidentally—the death needed to be atoned for by blood. Their "eye for an eye, tooth for a tooth" culture permitted a victim's next of kin to take the life of the perpetrator—even if the death was accidental. These cities, then, provided a necessary sanctuary for the person who accidentally killed another person. The person who fled here was required to remain in the city of refuge until the death of the high priest (Numbers 35:28).

The photograph on this page shows the landscapes of Kadesh, near the city of refuge for the northern area of Israel.

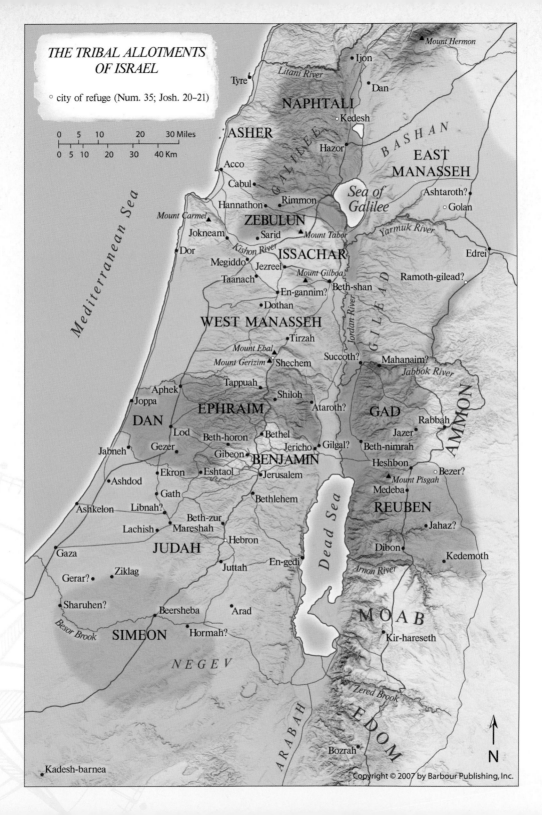

THE TRIBAL ALLOTMENTS
OF ISRAEL

○ city of refuge (Num. 35; Josh. 20–21)

0   5   10   20   30 Miles
0 5 10   20   30   40 Km

Mount Hermon

Ijon

Litani River

Tyre

Dan

NAPHTALI

○ Kedesh

ASHER

Hazor

BASHAN

EAST
MANASSEH

Acco

Cabul

*Sea of
Galilee*

Ashtaroth?

○ Golan

Hannathon

Rimmon

Mount Carmel ▲

ZEBULUN

Yarmuk River

Jokneam

Sarid

▲ *Mount Tabor*

Edrei

Kishon River

Dor

Megiddo

ISSACHAR

Jezreel

Taanach

Mount Gilboa ▲

Beth-shan

Ramoth-gilead?

En-gannim?

Dothan

GILEAD

WEST MANASSEH

Tirzah

Mount Ebal ▲

Succoth?

Mahanaim?

Mount Gerizim ▲ Shechem

Jabbok River

Tappuah

AMMON

Aphek

Shiloh

Joppa

EPHRAIM

Ataroth?

GAD

Rabbah

DAN

Lod

Bethel

Jazer

Beth-horon

Jericho?

Gilgal?

Beth-nimrah

Gezer

Gibeon

BENJAMIN

Heshbon

Jabneh

Eshtaol

Bezer?

Ekron

Jerusalem

▲ *Mount Pisgah*

Ashdod

Gath

Medeba

Ashkelon

Libnah?

Bethlehem

REUBEN

Lachish

Beth-zur
Mareshah

Jahaz?

Gaza

Hebron

Dibon

Kedemoth

Gerar?

Ziklag

Juttah

En-gedi

Dead Sea

Arnon River

Sharuhen?

Beersheba

Arad

M O A B

Besor Brook

SIMEON

Hormah?

Kir-haresheth

N E G E V

Zered Brook

A R A B A H

E D O M

Bozrah

N ↑

Kadesh-barnea

Copyright © 2007 by Barbour Publishing, Inc.

Mediterranean Sea

Jordan River

JUDAH

41

ISRAEL DURING THE TIME OF THE JUDGES

Before kings ruled over the Israelites, they were led by leaders known as judges. These judges were known for their military leadership and for being led by God's Spirit. These judges would rise up for a time to combat a particular foe, and then later another would arise somewhere else for another purpose.

In the previous generations, Moses and Joshua had instructed the Israelites to conquer or drive out all native peoples from the land. As the years went by, the Israelites left a number of cities unconquered (these cities are marked in white on the map). These remaining peoples created problems for the Israelites by leading them astray with idolatry and other sins—and occasionally fighting them on the battlefield. Judges often served to lead the Israelite army to break the hold of these and other invading enemies.

Below is a list of biblical judges.

Judge	Biblical Reference	The Enemy They Fought
Othniel	Judges 3:9–11	Mesopotamia
Ehud	Judges 3:15–30	Moabites
Shamgar	Judges 3:31	Philistines
Deborah and Barak	Judges 4:4–5:31	Canaanites
Gideon	Judges 6:7–8:35	Midianites
Tola	Judges 10:1–2	None listed
Jair	Judges 10:3–5	None listed
Jephthah	Judges 10:6–12:7	Ammonites
Ibzan	Judges 12:8–10	None listed
Elon	Judges 12:11–12	None listed
Abdon	Judges 12:13–15	None listed
Samson	Judges 13:2–16:31	Philistines
Eli	1 Samuel 1–4	None listed
Samuel	1 Samuel 7–9	Philistines

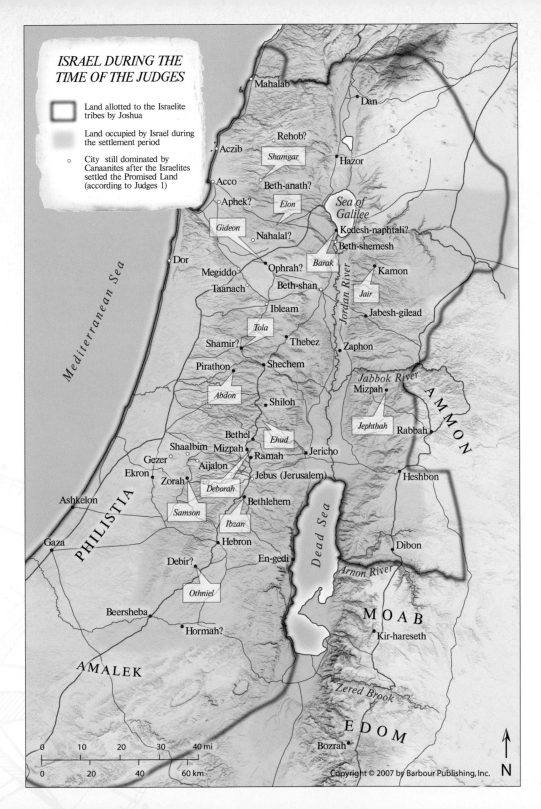

ISRAEL DURING THE TIME OF THE JUDGES

Land allotted to the Israelite tribes by Joshua

Land occupied by Israel during the settlement period

○ City still dominated by Canaanites after the Israelites settled the Promised Land (according to Judges 1)

Mahalab

Dan

Rehob?

Aczib

Hazor

Acco

Beth-anath?

Shamgar

Elon

Aphek?

Sea of Galilee

Gideon

Nahalal?

Kedesh-naphtali?

Beth-shemesh

Dor

Ophrah?

Barak

Kamon

Megiddo

Beth-shan

Jair

Taanach

Jabesh-gilead

Ibleam

Tola

Shamir?

Thebez

Zaphon

Pirathon

Shechem

Jabbok River

Mizpah

Abdon

Shiloh

Jephthah

Rabbah

AMMON

Bethel

Ehud

Shaalbim

Mizpah

Gezer

Ramah

Jericho

Aijalon

Ekron

Zorah

Jebus (Jerusalem)

Heshbon

Deborah

Ashkelon

PHILISTIA

Bethlehem

Samson

Ibzan

Dead Sea

Gaza

Hebron

Dibon

Debir?

En-gedi

Arnon River

Othniel

Beersheba

MOAB

Hormah?

Kir-hareseth

AMALEK

Zered Brook

EDOM

Bozrah

Mediterranean Sea

Jordan River

| 0 | 10 | 20 | 30 | 40 mi |

| 0 | 20 | 40 | 60 km |

Copyright © 2007 by Barbour Publishing, Inc.

N

43

DEBORAH AND BARAK DEFEAT THE CANAANITES

During the time of the judges, the Israelites repeatedly forgot the Lord and His promises in a regular cycle of sin, punishment, repentance, and deliverance. First, the people abandoned God and sinned against Him. God then delivered them into the hands of their enemies. Eventually the people turned back to God, crying out for deliverance. Finally, God appointed a judge to lead them to victory over their enemies. Soon afterward, however, the people turned away from God once more and the cycle began again.

During Deborah's time, Jabin, a king of Canaan, conquered the Israelites. When the people repented, God appointed Deborah (a prophetess of God and Israel's only female judge) and Barak (her military general) to lead the way. While Barak drew his army primarily from the nearby northern tribes of Zebulun and Naphtali, the battle force also included men from the tribes of Ephraim, Benjamin, and Manasseh. Barak's army assembled to confront the Canaanites at Mount Tabor (pictured on this page).

This mountain, a little more than ten miles from the Sea of Galilee, became the staging ground of the Israelites. With God's help, Barak and his army of ten thousand foot soldiers routed the chariot army of Jabin. (Read the story of the battle and Deborah's victory song in Judges 4–5.)

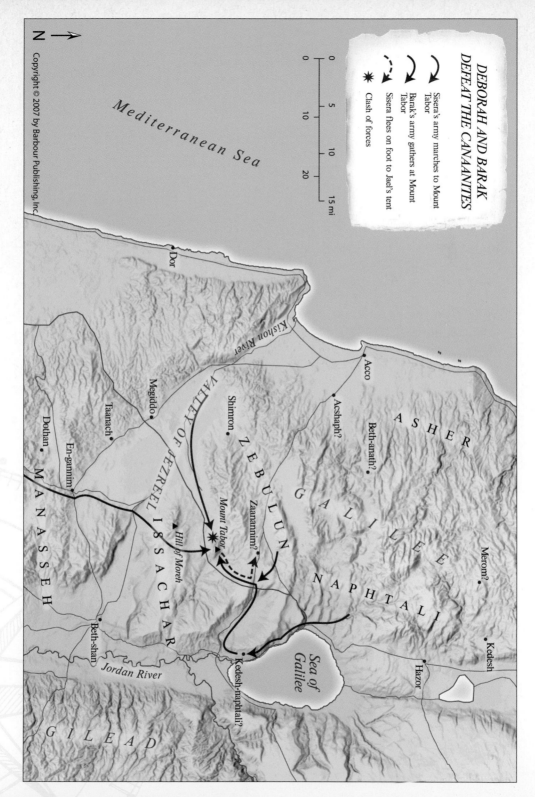

N →

Copyright © 2007 by Barbour Publishing, Inc.

DEBORAH AND BARAK
DEFEAT THE CANAANITES

Sisera's army marches to Mount Tabor

Barak's army gathers at Mount Tabor

Sisera flees on foot to Jael's tent

Clash of forces

0

0   5   10   20   15 mi

Mediterranean Sea

Dor

Kishon River

Acco

VALLEY OF JEZREEL

Megiddo

Taanach

Shimron

Acshaph?

Beth-anath?

ASHER

Dothan

En-gannim

Zaanannim?

ZEBULUN

GALILEE

Merom?

M A N A S S E H

I S S A C H A R

Hill of Moreh

Mount Tabor

NAPHTALI

Beth-shan

Jordan River

Kedesh-naphtali?

Sea of Galilee

Hazor

Kedesh

G I L E A D

GIDEON DEFEATS THE MIDIANITES

The story of Gideon opens with God's people beginning the predictable cycle found so often in Judges: "Again the Israelites did evil in the eyes of the Lord" (6:1). This time, God handed them over to serve the Midianites for seven years.

In anointing Gideon as Israel's next judge, God selected an unlikely hero. By Gideon's own account, he came from an insignificant family. In addition to his insignificant heritage, Gideon's own personality seemed to lack the confidence and assertiveness we would normally expect to find in a leader.

When Gideon finally accepted the mission and trusted God for the result, God put that trust to the test by reducing the size of Gideon's large army to a tiny force of three hundred men. At the Valley of Jezreel near the hill of Moreh (see photo), God, Gideon, and the small army used creative battle tactics to route the Midianite army and chase them deep into the Arabian Desert.

By using an unlikely hero and unlikely methods, God made sure He received the credit for routing another enemy from the land of Israel (Judges 6–8).

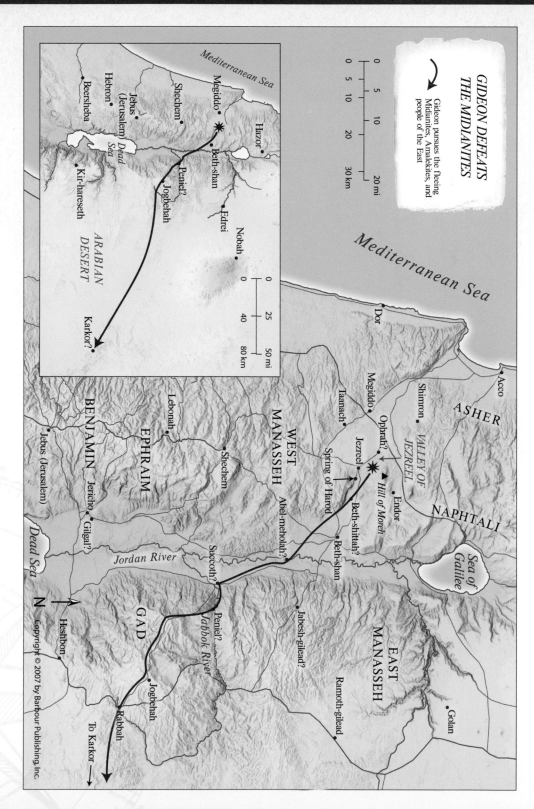

GIDEON DEFEATS
THE MIDIANITES

Gideon pursues the fleeing
Midianites, Amalekites, and
people of the East

Mediterranean Sea

0   5   10   20   30 km
0   5   10   20 mi

Inset map labels:
Mediterranean Sea
Hazor
Megiddo
Shechem
Beth-shan
Peniel?
Jogbehah
Edrei
Nobah
(Jerusalem) Jebus
Hebron
Beersheba
Kir-hareseth
Dead Sea
ARABIAN DESERT
Karkor?

0   25   40   50 mi
0   40   80 km

Main map labels:
Mediterranean Sea
Acco
Dor
ASHER
Shimron
Megiddo
Taanach
VALLEY OF JEZREEL
Ophrah?
Jezreel
NAPHTALI
Spring of Harod
Endor
Hill of Moreh
Beth-shittah?
Beth-shan
Sea of Galilee
WEST MANASSEH
Abel-meholah?
Lebonah
EPHRAIM
Shechem
BENJAMIN
Jabesh-gilead?
Succoth?
Jordan River
Jebus (Jerusalem)
Jericho?
Gilgal?
EAST MANASSEH
Ramoth-gilead
Golan
Dead Sea
N
Peniel?
Jabbok River
GAD
Heshbon
Jogbehah
Rabbah
To Karkor

JEPHTHAH DEFEATS THE AMMONITES

The people of Israel found themselves facing a familiar enemy when the Ammonites initiated a land dispute and moved westward to reclaim land they felt rightfully belonged to them. Hearing His people call for help, God selected another unlikely candidate for the job of judge—Jephthah, the son of a prostitute (Judges 11:1).

Jephthah, whose father was Gilead, grew into a strong man and a skilled soldier. However, since he lived in a culture where heritage mattered, Jephthah's stepbrothers drove him away and Jephthah settled in Tob.

After the Ammonites attacked the people of Israel, the elders began to search for the right leader to lead the military campaign against their enemies. Remembering Jephthah, the elders traveled to Tob, convinced him to take the leadership position, and brought him back to his people.

Filled with the Spirit of God, Jephthah led an attack, pushed south, and won victories against twenty cities. (During this series of battles Jephthah also made a reckless vow. See Judges 11:29–40 for details.) After winning an important and decisive battle, Jephthah was greeted not with cheers and accolades but with hostility from his fellow countrymen. Angry that they had not participated in the battle (and therefore missed out on its plunder), men from the tribe of Ephraim blamed Jephthah. Tensions escalated until war broke out at Zaphon, where Jephthah easily defeated his opponents. The story of the Ammonites' invasion and Jephthah can be read in Judges 10–12.

The photo on this page is of a tower built by the Ammonites.

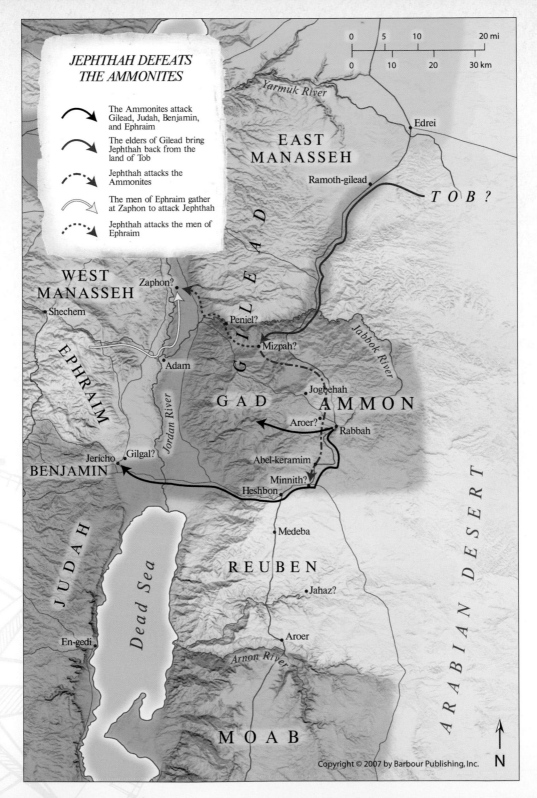

JEPHTHAH DEFEATS THE AMMONITES

→ The Ammonites attack Gilead, Judah, Benjamin, and Ephraim

→ The elders of Gilead bring Jephthah back from the land of Tob

⇢ Jephthah attacks the Ammonites

⇨ The men of Ephraim gather at Zaphon to attack Jephthah

⇢ Jephthah attacks the men of Ephraim

0   5   10   20 mi
0   10   20   30 km

Yarmuk River

Edrei

EAST MANASSEH

Ramoth-gilead

TOB ?

WEST MANASSEH

Zaphon?

Shechem

Peniel?

G I L E A D

Jabbok River

Mizpah?

Adam

Jordan River

G A D

Jogbehah

AMMON

EPHRAIM

Aroer?   Rabbah

Jericho   Gilgal?

BENJAMIN

Abel-keramim

Minnith?

Heshbon

Dead Sea

Medeba

REUBEN

J U D A H

Jahaz?

En-gedi

Aroer

Arnon River

A R A B I A N   D E S E R T

M O A B

N

Copyright © 2007 by Barbour Publishing, Inc.

49

SAMSON'S DEEDS AND ISRAEL'S ATTACK OF GIBEAH

Somewhere between Zorah and Eshtaol lies the location of Samson's birth and burial. While the exact spot is unknown, this photograph highlights the traditional site of his tomb.

Samson's life and death were both characterized by self-imposed tragedy, beginning with an ill-advised decision to marry a Philistine woman. (His journey into the Philistine area is marked by red on the map.) Before his honeymoon ended, Samson traveled to Ashkelon where he killed and plundered thirty Philistines to pay off a wager made during his wedding feast. When Samson returned to reconcile his debt, he learned that his new wife had been given in marriage to someone else (Judges 14). In revenge, he destroyed a large portion of the Philistine crops. Before the Philistines could exact punishment, Samson single-handedly killed one thousand of them with the jawbone of a donkey at Lehi (Judges 15).

Later, he visited the heart of the Philistine country in Gaza and spent the night with a prostitute. When the men of Gaza prepared to capture him, Samson escaped by ripping out the city gates, which he carried to the Israelite city of Hebron (as indicated by the dotted red lines and found in Judges 16).

Betrayed by Delilah and finally captured by the Philistines, Samson refocused his heart on God. He used his great strength to push down the building where he was held prisoner—killing himself as well as his Philistine captors.

While God used Samson to break the Philistines' hold over Israel, God was also concerned enough with the spiritual state of His people to discipline them as necessary. The blue and yellow lines recount a gruesome story from Judges 20 involving the Benjamites; when they had sinned, the remaining tribes of Israel inflicted a harsh punishment on their brothers. These stories illustrate how the days of the judges were marked by darkness and violence.

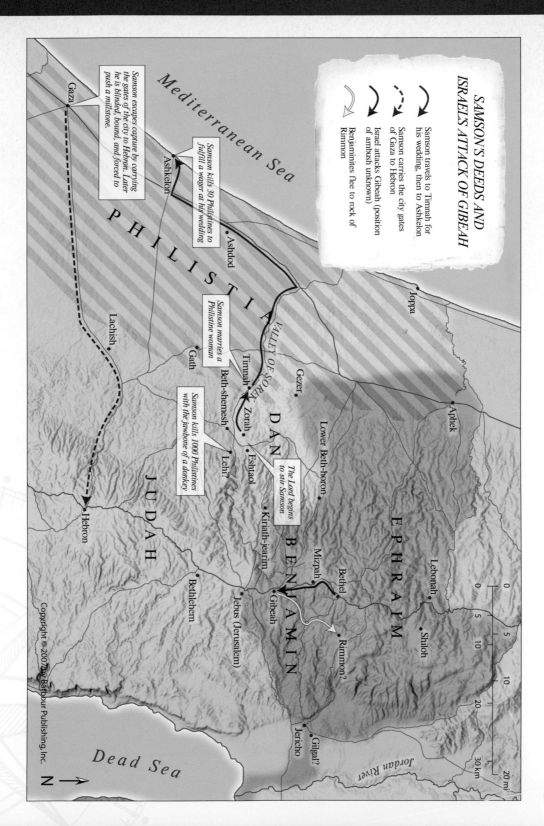

SAMSON'S DEEDS AND ISRAEL'S ATTACK OF GIBEAH

Samson travels to Timnah for his wedding, then to Ashkelon

Samson carries the city gates of Gaza to Hebron

Israel attacks Gibeah (position of ambush unknown)

Benjaminites flee to rock of Rimmon

Samson escapes capture by carrying the gates of the city to Hebron. Later he is blinded, bound, and forced to push a millstone.

Samson kills 30 Philistines to fulfill a wager at his wedding

Samson marries a Philistine woman

Samson kills 1000 Philistines with the jawbone of a donkey

The Lord begins to stir Samson

Mediterranean Sea

PHILISTIA

JUDAH

DAN

BENJAMIN

EPHRAIM

Dead Sea

Jordan River

VALLEY OF SOREK

Gaza

Ashkelon

Ashdod

Joppa

Lachish

Gath

Gezer

Aphek

Timnah

Beth-shemesh

Zorah

Lehi?

Eshtaol

Lower Beth-horon

Kiriath-jearim

Mizpah

Bethel

Lebonah

Shiloh

Hebron

Bethlehem

Jebus (Jerusalem)

Gibeah

Rimmon?

Jericho

Gilgal?

N →

0   5   10   20   30 km

0   5   10   20 mi

THE ARK OF THE COVENANT IS CAPTURED AND RETURNED

God had commissioned the Ark of the Covenant (see photo of replica) as a tangible reminder of His power and presence. Designed to induce awe and respect, the ark was most often kept in the tabernacle—the center of Israelite worship.

During the days of Eli the priest, the Israelites experienced military defeat against the Philistines (1 Samuel 4). Desperately looking for a way to secure victory, Eli's sons led the Israelites into battle while carrying the Ark of the Covenant as a lucky charm.

God's presence, however, depended not upon the Ark of the Covenant but upon the God of the covenant—and the Israelites' attempt to secure a victory apart from faithfulness to the covenant failed. Eli's sons were killed at Ebenezer, and the Philistines captured the ark, putting the sacred box in the temple of Dagon. To their dismay, every place the Philistines brought the ark, God demonstrated His power by bringing them misfortune (1 Samuel 5). Finally, in an effort to rid themselves of the terrible plagues, the Philistines put the ark on a cart and sent the oxen back within Israel's borders (1 Samuel 6).

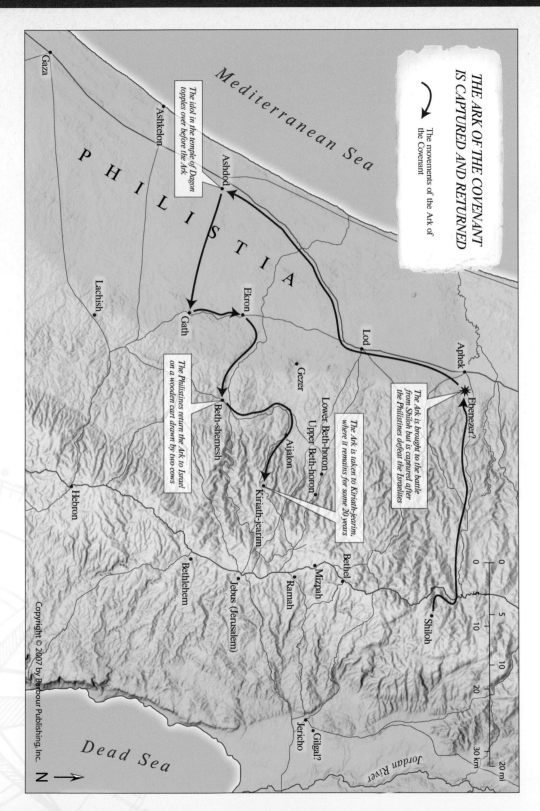

THE ARK OF THE COVENANT
IS CAPTURED AND RETURNED

The movements of the Ark of
the Covenant

Mediterranean Sea

PHILISTIA

Gaza

Ashkelon

Ashdod

The idol in the temple of Dagon
topples over before the Ark

Lachish

Ekron

Gath

Gezer

Lod

Aphek

Ebenezer?

The Ark is brought to the battle
from Shiloh but is captured after
the Philistines defeat the Israelites

The Ark is taken to Kiriath-jearim,
where it remains for some 20 years

Lower Beth-horon
Upper Beth-horon

The Philistines return the Ark to Israel
on a wooden cart drawn by two cows

Beth-shemesh

Aijalon

Kiriath-jearim

Bethel

Mizpah

Ramah

Shiloh

Hebron

Bethlehem

Jebus (Jerusalem)

Jericho

Gilgal?

Jordan River

Dead Sea

N →

0   5   10   20 mi

0   5   10   20   30 km

ISRAEL DURING THE TIME OF SAUL

The events at the beginning of Saul's reign helped Saul solidify his leadership: Though Samuel had already anointed him as king (1 Samuel 10), Saul had not assumed kingship with a grandiose display of power. Instead of acting as Israel's new leader, Saul returned to his home and was plowing his fields when the Ammonites attacked Jabesh Gilead (1 Samuel 11). Saul left his fields, mustered 330,000 men at Bezek, and easily defeated the enemy at Jabesh Gilead. The people celebrated the event by renewing Saul's kingship at Gilgal.

Later, Saul and his son Jonathan won a decisive battle against the Philistines. The turning point for the battle came at Michmash, where "Jonathan climbed up, using his hands and feet, with his armor-bearer right behind him. The Philistines fell before Jonathan, and his armor-bearer followed and killed behind him" (1 Samuel 14:13). Jonathan's remarkable victory over the Philistine outpost occurred near these rough cliffs (see photo and inset map). On this rocky crag, the prince and his armor-bearer climbed difficult terrain to lead the Israelite army to a surprising victory (read the story in 1 Samuel 14).

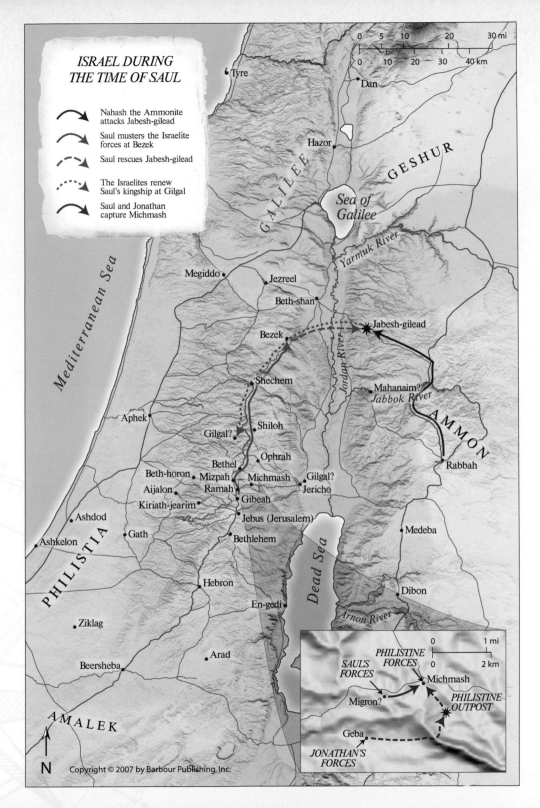

ISRAEL DURING THE TIME OF SAUL

Nahash the Ammonite attacks Jabesh-gilead

Saul musters the Israelite forces at Bezek

Saul rescues Jabesh-gilead

The Israelites renew Saul's kingship at Gilgal

Saul and Jonathan capture Michmash

Tyre

Dan

Mediterranean Sea

GALILEE

GESHUR

Hazor

Sea of Galilee

Yarmuk River

Megiddo

Jezreel

Beth-shan

Bezek

Jabesh-gilead

Shechem

Jordan River

Mahanaim?
Jabbok River

AMMON

Aphek

Gilgal?

Shiloh

Ophrah

Bethel

Beth-horon

Mizpah

Michmash

Gilgal?

Rabbah

Aijalon

Ramah

Jericho

Kiriath-jearim

Gibeah

Ashdod

Jebus (Jerusalem)

Gath

Medeba

Ashkelon

PHILISTIA

Bethlehem

Dead Sea

Hebron

Ziklag

En-gedi

Dibon

Arnon River

Arad

Beersheba

AMALEK

N

Copyright © 2007 by Barbour Publishing, Inc.

Inset map

0 — 1 mi
0 — 2 km

SAUL'S FORCES

PHILISTINE FORCES

Michmash

Migron?

PHILISTINE OUTPOST

Geba

JONATHAN'S FORCES

DAVID AND SAUL: FROM GIBEAH TO THE STRONGHOLD

David's military success (see inset and 1 Samuel 17–18) and popularity with the people ended up forcing him to spend many years on the lam running from a jealous King Saul. Rather than fight the king directly and risk harming God's anointed leader, David evaded him by moving from

place to place. However, God used this time to prepare David for his future career as king and commander-in-chief of the Israelite army. The map to the right highlights eight stops David made as he moved to avoid confrontation with Saul.

Location	Biblical Reference	Key Event
Gibeah	1 Samuel 19:11	David is rescued by his wife Michal (the daughter of Saul).
Ramah	1 Samuel 19:18	David meets with the prophet Samuel.
Gibeah	1 Samuel 20:42	Jonathan (the son of Saul) warns David of trouble.
Nob	1 Samuel 21:1	The priest gives David the sword of Goliath.
Gath	1 Samuel 21:10	David escapes harm by pretending to be insane.
Adullam	1 Samuel 22:1	David gathers 400 men (see photo of location).
Mizpah	1 Samuel 22:3–4	David places his parents in the care of the king of Moab.
The Stronghold	1 Samuel 22:4	David waits for God's instruction.

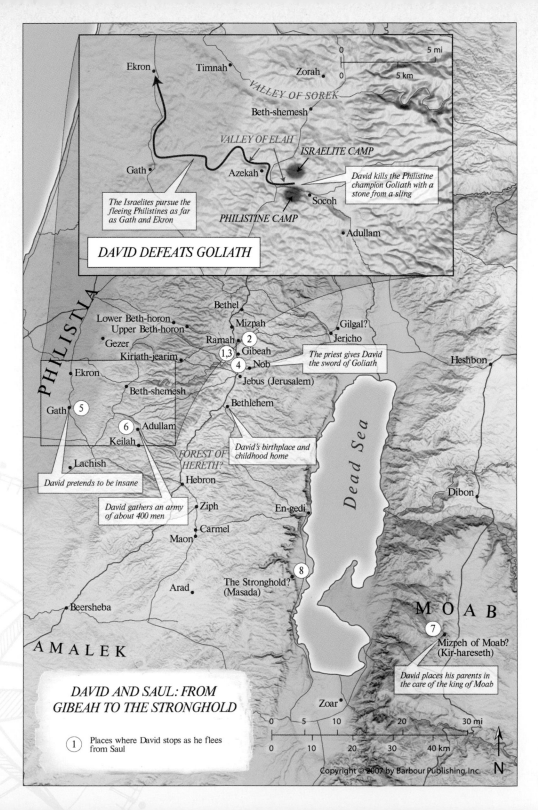

DAVID DEFEATS GOLIATH

Ekron   Timnah   Zorah

0   5 mi
0   5 km

VALLEY OF SOREK

Beth-shemesh

VALLEY OF ELAH

ISRAELITE CAMP

Gath

Azekah

David kills the Philistine
champion Goliath with a
stone from a sling

Socoh

The Israelites pursue the
fleeing Philistines as far
as Gath and Ekron

PHILISTINE CAMP

Adullam

Bethel

Lower Beth-horon   Mizpah   Gilgal?

Upper Beth-horon   Ramah   Jericho

PHILISTIA

Gezer   ①,③   Gibeah

Kiriath-jearim   ④   Nob

The priest gives David
the sword of Goliath

Ekron

Beth-shemesh   Jebus (Jerusalem)   Heshbon

Gath   ⑤   Bethlehem

Dead Sea

⑥   Adullam

Keilah

David's birthplace and
childhood home

*FOREST OF
HERETH?*

Lachish   Hebron

David pretends to be insane

Ziph

David gathers an army
of about 400 men

Carmel   En-gedi

Maon

Dibon

⑧

Arad   The Stronghold?
(Masada)

Beersheba

M O A B

A M A L E K

⑦

Mizpeh of Moab?
(Kir-hareseth)

*DAVID AND SAUL: FROM
GIBEAH TO THE STRONGHOLD*

David places his parents in
the care of the king of Moab

①   Places where David stops as he flees
from Saul

Zoar

0   5   10   20   30 mi

0   10   20   30   40 km

N

DAVID AND SAUL: FROM THE STRONG-HOLD TO ZIKLAG

David's flight from Saul lasted many years. Below are additional places David sought refuge.

Location	Biblical Reference	Key Event
The Stronghold	1 Samuel 22:4	David waits for God's instruction.
Forest of Hereth	1 Samuel 22:5	The prophet Gad sends David to hide here.
Keilah	1 Samuel 23:1–2	David rescues Keilah from the Philistine invaders.
Ziph	1 Samuel 23:14–24	David meets Jonathan and then is betrayed by the men of Ziph.
Desert of Maon	1 Samuel 23:25	David narrowly escapes capture when Saul cuts off pursuit because of the invading Philistine army.
En-Gedi	1 Samuel 24:1	David resists the opportunity to kill Saul while resting in a cave (see photo of En Gedi caves).
The Stronghold	1 Samuel 24:22	David rests here after pledging new allegiance to Saul.
Desert of Maon	1 Samuel 25–26	Nabal insults David. David meets Abigail and turns down a second chance to kill Saul.
Gath	1 Samuel 27:2	David seeks asylum with Achish.
Ziklag	1 Samuel 27:6	Achish gives David a home in the city of Ziklag.

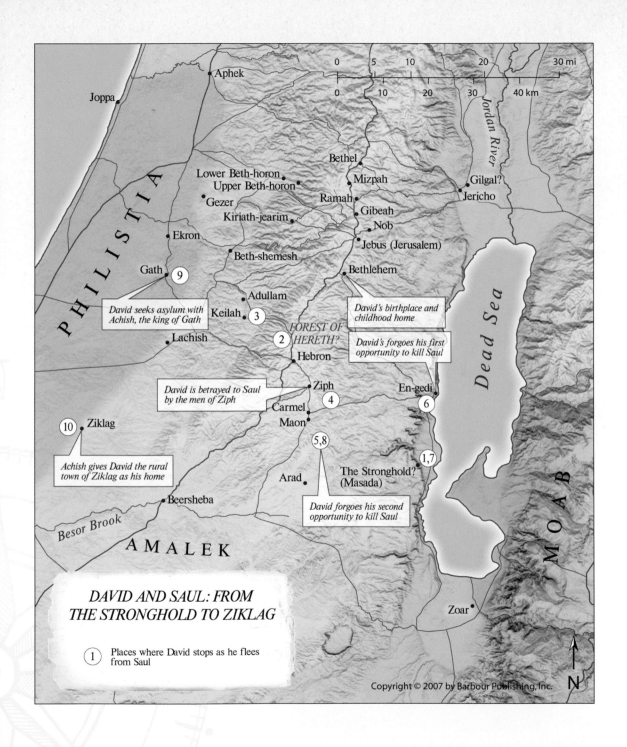

Joppa

Aphek

PHILISTIA

Lower Beth-horon
Upper Beth-horon
Gezer
Kiriath-jearim

Ekron

Beth-shemesh

Gath ⑨

*David seeks asylum with
Achish, the king of Gath*

Adullam

Keilah ③

Lachish

② *FOREST OF
HERETH?*

Hebron

*David is betrayed to Saul
by the men of Ziph*

Ziph

④

Carmel
Maon

⑩ Ziklag

*Achish gives David the rural
town of Ziklag as his home*

⑤,⑧

Arad

Beersheba

Besor Brook

AMALEK

Bethel

Mizpah
Ramah
Gibeah
Nob

Jebus (Jerusalem)

Bethlehem

*David's birthplace and
childhood home*

*David's forgoes his first
opportunity to kill Saul*

En-gedi

⑥

①,⑦

The Stronghold?
(Masada)

*David forgoes his second
opportunity to kill Saul*

Gilgal?
Jericho

Jordan River

Dead Sea

MOAB

Zoar

DAVID AND SAUL: FROM
THE STRONGHOLD TO ZIKLAG

① Places where David stops as he flees
from Saul

N

Copyright © 2007 by Barbour Publishing, Inc.

DAVID PURSUES THE AMALEKITES

While David lived in Philistine territory, he feigned loyalty to their king and fabricated stories about how he had harmed the people of Judah (1 Samuel 27). When the Philistines marched north to attack Saul at Aphek, David even followed in an apparent act of solidarity. After the other commanders expressed their distrust that David would fight his own countrymen, King Achish sent David home.

Once David and his army of six hundred men arrived back at Ziklag (see photo of location), they discovered that the Amalekites had attacked the city and carried off all the remaining residents as captives. (The Amalekites had hassled Israel in previous generations. See Exodus 17 and Judges 6.)

David pursued the Amalekite raiding party, defeated them, and brought everyone back home safely. Rather than keeping the plunder they obtained from the Amalekites, David built goodwill by sending gifts to a number of cities across the southern part of Israel. (Read the story in 1 Samuel 30.)

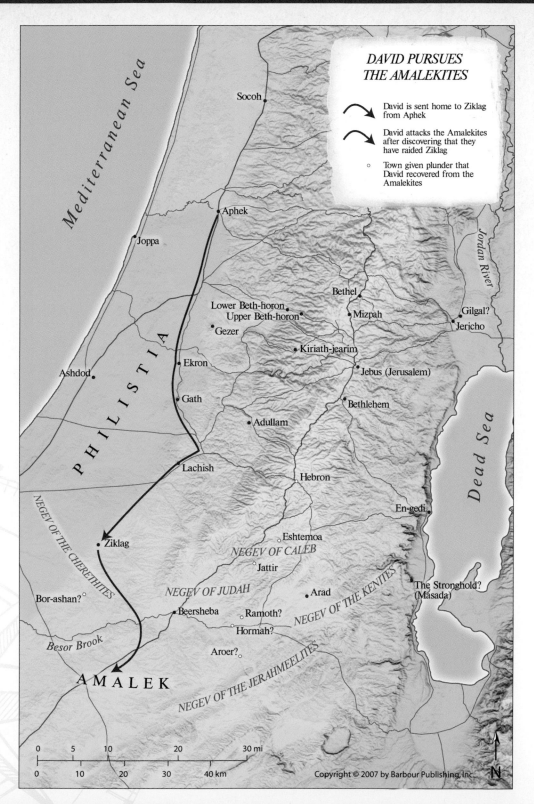

DAVID PURSUES THE AMALEKITES

David is sent home to Ziklag from Aphek

David attacks the Amalekites after discovering that they have raided Ziklag

Town given plunder that David recovered from the Amalekites

Mediterranean Sea

Socoh

Joppa

Aphek

PHILISTIA

Bethel

Lower Beth-horon
Upper Beth-horon

Mizpah

Gilgal?

Jericho

Gezer

Kiriath-jearim

Ekron

Jebus (Jerusalem)

Ashdod

Gath

Bethlehem

Adullam

Jordan River

Dead Sea

Lachish

Hebron

En-gedi

Ziklag

Eshtemoa

NEGEV OF CALEB

NEGEV OF THE CHERETHITES

Jattir

The Stronghold?
(Masada)

NEGEV OF JUDAH

Arad

NEGEV OF THE KENITES

Bor-ashan?

Beersheba

Ramoth?

Hormah?

Besor Brook

Aroer?

AMALEK

NEGEV OF THE JERAHMEELITES

| 0 | 5 | 10 | 20 | 30 mi |
| 0 | 10 | 20 | 30 | 40 km |

Copyright © 2007 by Barbour Publishing, Inc.

N

THE BATTLE AT MOUNT GILBOA

Apparently King Saul sensed that God's blessing had left him and that the looming battle against the Philistines would end in disaster. With the army assembled in Jezreel, Saul secretly met with the witch of Endor in an effort to communicate with Samuel through an ancient séance. Saul indeed saw a vision of Samuel, which only confirmed his fear of imminent doom (1 Samuel 28).

At the beginning of the battle, the Philistines drove the Israelites south to Mt. Gilboa (see photo). With their backs against the mountain, Saul and his son Jonathan died (1 Samuel 31).

When Saul first became king, he solidified his leadership by rescuing the town of Jabesh-gilead from an invading army (see page 55). Now, at the end of his life, the people of this town honored their late king and his sons by traveling through the night to rescue their abused bodies and honorably cremate their remains.

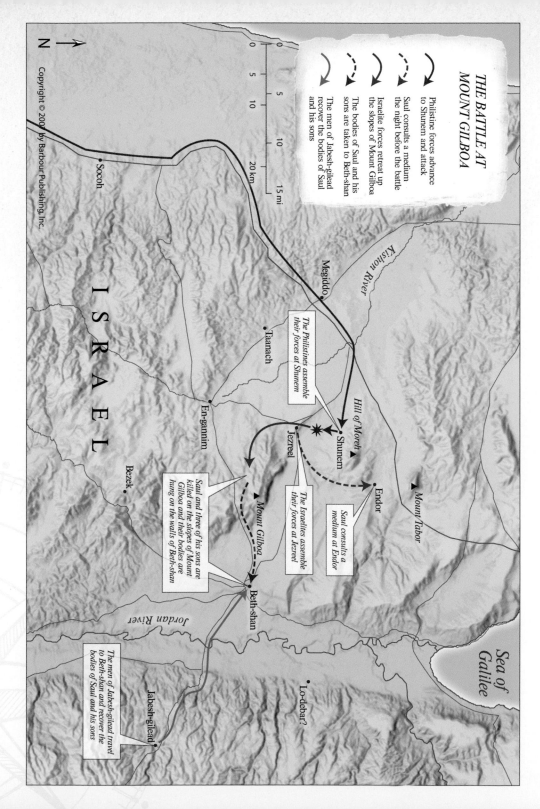

THE BATTLE AT
MOUNT GILBOA

Philistine forces advance
to Shunem and attack

Saul consults a medium
the night before the battle

Israelite forces retreat up
the slopes of Mount Gilboa

The bodies of Saul and his
sons are taken to Beth-shan

The men of Jabesh-gilead
recover the bodies of Saul
and his sons

N

0 ─────
0 ─────
        5
5 ─────
       10
10 ─────

20 km

15 mi

Copyright © 2007 by Barbour Publishing, Inc.

I S R A E L

Socoh

Megiddo

Kishon River

Taanach

En-gannim

Bezek

Hill of Moreh

*The Philistines assemble
their forces at Shunem*

Jezreel

Shunem

Mount Tabor

Endor

*Saul consults a
medium at Endor*

*The Israelites assemble
their forces at Jezreel*

Mount Gilboa

*Saul and three of his sons are
killed on the slopes of Mount
Gilboa and their bodies are
hung on the walls of Beth-shan*

Jordan River

Beth-shan

Sea of
Galilee

Lo-debar?

*The men of Jabesh-gilead travel
to Beth-shan and recover the
bodies of Saul and his sons*

Jabesh-gilead

DAVID SECURES HIS REIGN OVER ISRAEL

The transition from Saul's kingship to David's reign was neither simple nor swift. Following typical rules of succession, the people first appointed Saul's son Ish-bosheth as king (2 Samuel 2:10). Only the tribe of Judah looked to David as their new king.

For two years, civil war existed between David and his army (led by Joab) and Ish-bosheth and his army (led by Abner). The conflict was highlighted by a bloody battle at the pool of Gibeon (see photograph of this location below and read the story in 2 Samuel 2).

The war came to an end quickly when conflict arose between Ish-bosheth and Abner. After an internal power struggle, Abner defected and pledged his allegiance to David (2 Samuel 3). With Ish-bosheth's primary protector gone, the son of Saul was assassinated—having reigned for two years.

Rather than look to another member of Saul's house to lead them, the people of Israel finally united under David and pledged allegiance to their new king (2 Samuel 5).

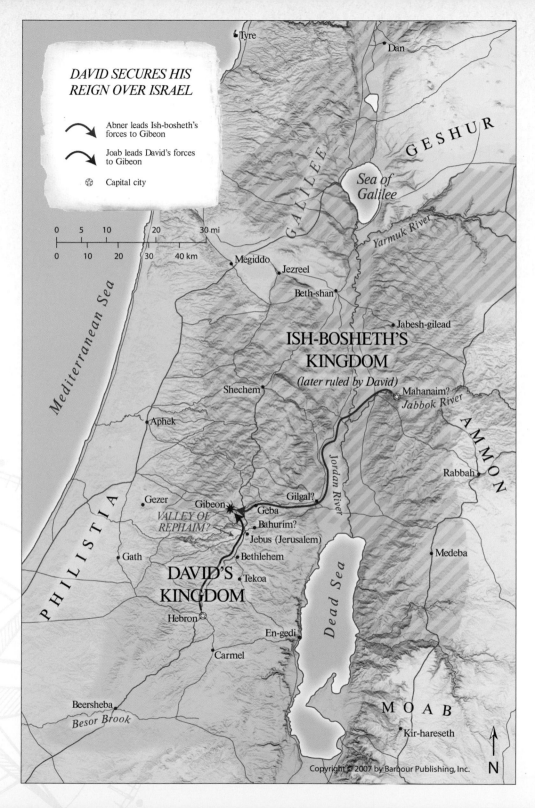

DAVID SECURES HIS
REIGN OVER ISRAEL

Abner leads Ish-bosheth's
forces to Gibeon

Joab leads David's forces
to Gibeon

Capital city

Tyre

Dan

GESHUR

GALILEE

Sea of
Galilee

Yarmuk River

0   5   10   20   30 mi
0   10   20   30   40 km

Megiddo

Jezreel

Beth-shan

Mediterranean Sea

Jabesh-gilead

ISH-BOSHETH'S
KINGDOM

(later ruled by David)

Shechem

Mahanaim?
Jabbok River

Aphek

AMMON

Jordan River

Rabbah

Gezer

Gibeon

Gilgal?

VALLEY OF
REPHAIM?

Geba

Bahurim?

Jebus (Jerusalem)

Gath

Bethlehem

Medeba

DAVID'S
KINGDOM

Tekoa

PHILISTIA

Hebron

Dead Sea

En-gedi

Carmel

MOAB

Beersheba

Besor Brook

Kir-hareseth

N

DAVID DEFEATS THE AMMONITES AND THE ARAMEANS

David's reign as king began with a series of military victories (see 2 Samuel 5, 8). In these conflicts, David defeated hostile neighbors to the west (the Philistines) and to the southeast (the Moabites). The Ammonites, his neighbors to the east, faced the choice of living peacefully with their neighbors or going to war with them.

When the king of Ammon died, David sent an envoy to express condolences to the new king. Rather than accept these men peacefully, the new king (Hanun) suspected the men of espionage. He treated them harshly, shaving half their beards and tearing their garments. These humiliated men stayed at Jericho until their beards grew back (2 Samuel 10).

When the Ammonites realized that war was imminent, they hired twenty thousand Aramean soldiers to help join the battle against David. Their effort to open a second front failed as David and his military commanders routed their enemies and subdued their neighbors to the east.

The photo shows the remains of a fort near Medeba that would have been in use around the time of this battle.

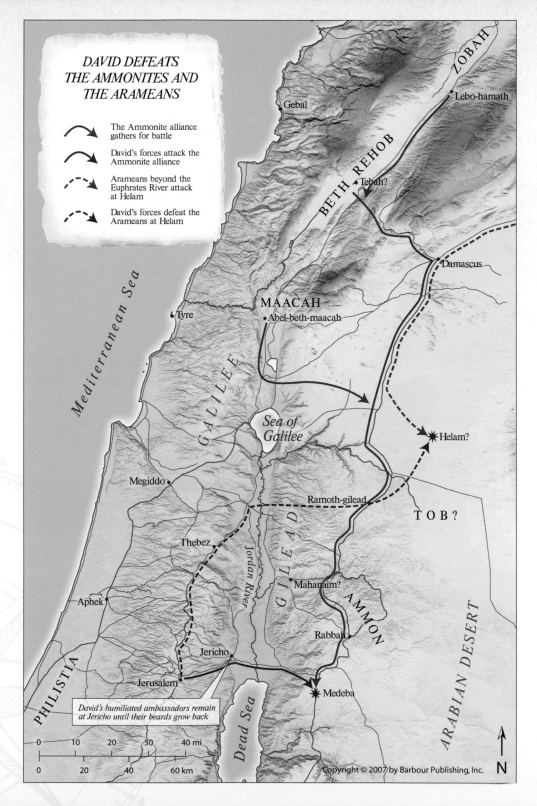

DAVID DEFEATS THE AMMONITES AND THE ARAMEANS

→ The Ammonite alliance gathers for battle

→ David's forces attack the Ammonite alliance

⇢ Arameans beyond the Euphrates River attack at Helam

⇢ David's forces defeat the Arameans at Helam

ZOBAH

Lebo-hamath

Gebal

BETH REHOB

Tebah?

Damascus

Mediterranean Sea

MAACAH

Tyre

Abel-beth-maacah

GALILEE

Sea of Galilee

Helam?

Megiddo

Ramoth-gilead

TOB?

Thebez

Jordan River

GILEAD

Mahanaim?

AMMON

Aphek

ARABIAN DESERT

Rabbah

Jericho

Jerusalem

David's humiliated ambassadors remain at Jericho until their beards grow back

Dead Sea

PHILISTIA

Medeba

| 0 | 10 | 20 | 30 | 40 mi |

| 0 | 20 | 40 | 60 km |

Copyright © 2007 by Barbour Publishing, Inc.

N

THE EXTENT OF DAVID'S KINGDOM

When Saul began his reign, the kingdom was a loose confederation of tribes rather than a well-organized, nationalistic kingdom. Over time, the monarchy's authority became more centralized and additional territory was added to the kingdom.

When David became king (2 Samuel 5), he made Jerusalem the new capital city. This "City of David" became both the civil and religious capital of the land. Remains of David's fortress have recently been found and are currently being excavated (see photo of the work in progress).

With a growing organization and structure to his government and military, David defeated the Philistines, Moabites, Ammonites, Arameans, and Edomites. As the population of Israel grew, David secured and expanded Israel's borders. This resulted in a country whose boundaries more closely matched God's promises given through Moses and Joshua.

Solomon became king and continued to organize the country of Israel. He used a conscripted labor force to complete magnificent building projects, accumulated vast wealth through domination of the trade routes, and ruled through a peaceful time (1 Kings 4:24). By historical accounts, the kingdom of Israel was more powerful and better organized than the surrounding peoples of this era, allowing its boundaries to continue to grow during a fairly peaceful time.

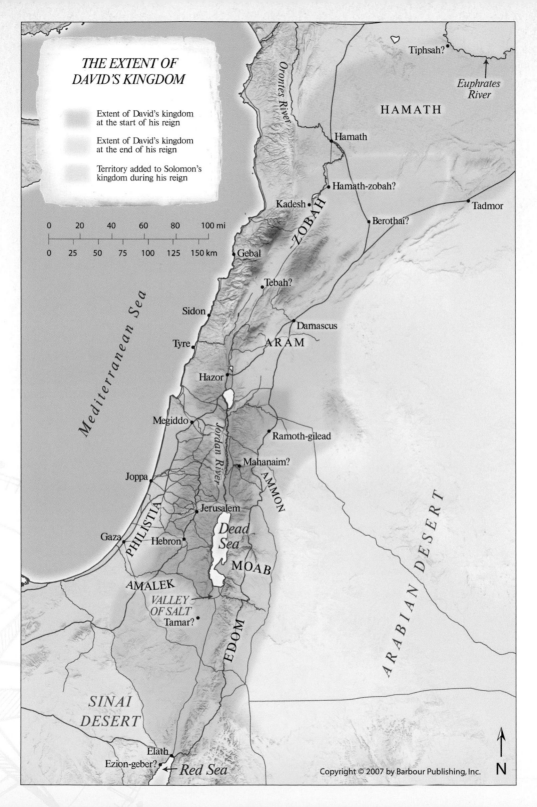

THE EXTENT OF DAVID'S KINGDOM

Extent of David's kingdom at the start of his reign

Extent of David's kingdom at the end of his reign

Territory added to Solomon's kingdom during his reign

0   20   40   60   80   100 mi

0   25   50   75   100   125   150 km

Tiphsah?

Euphrates River

HAMATH

Hamath

Orontes River

Hamath-zobah?

Kadesh

ZOBAH

Berothai?

Tadmor

Gebal

Tebah?

Sidon

Damascus

Tyre

ARAM

Hazor

Mediterranean Sea

Megiddo

Ramoth-gilead

Jordan River

Mahanaim?

Joppa

AMMON

Jerusalem

Dead Sea

Gaza

PHILISTIA

Hebron

MOAB

AMALEK

VALLEY OF SALT

Tamar?

EDOM

ARABIAN DESERT

SINAI DESERT

Elath

Ezion-geber?   ← *Red Sea*

Copyright © 2007 by Barbour Publishing, Inc.

N

ABSALOM'S REBELLION

Though often remembered for his many strengths, David was also a man with many weaknesses. The disarray of his family gave evidence of this. When his son Amnon raped his own half-sister, Tamar, David failed to address it. So his son Absalom took matters in his own hands and  killed his step-brother Amnon. Absalom then fled to Geshur (see photo of what may have been the capital of this region). He stayed in this area with his mother's family while living in exile.

After three years, David's general, Joab, recruited a woman to manipulate the king into lifting the prince's banishment. After Absalom returned to Jerusalem, David extended his forgiveness (2 Samuel 14). Rather than being grateful for this welcome, Absalom worked at stealing away the hearts of the people and eventually set himself up as king in Hebron—the former seat of David's throne. This location made a symbolic statement while also providing a practical location for rallying support.

Upon hearing of Absalom's ambitions and growing support, David fled from Jerusalem. The armies of both men finally clashed in the Forest of Ephraim, resulting in Absalom's death and David's return to Jerusalem. (The full story of Absalom and his rebellion can be found in 2 Samuel 13–18.)

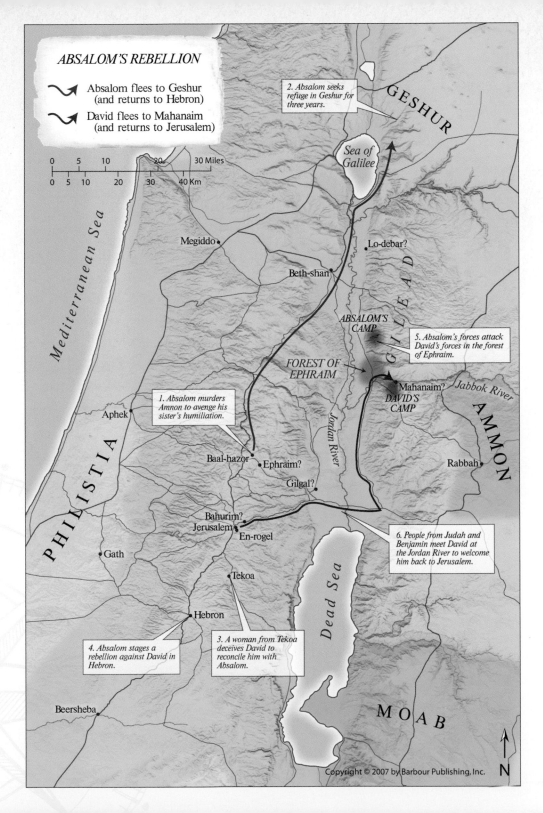

ABSALOM'S REBELLION

Absalom flees to Geshur
(and returns to Hebron)

David flees to Mahanaim
(and returns to Jerusalem)

0   5   10   20   30 Miles
0 5 10   20   30   40 Km

GESHUR

2. Absalom seeks refuge in Geshur for three years.

Sea of Galilee

Mediterranean Sea

Megiddo

Lo-debar?

Beth-shan

GILEAD

ABSALOM'S CAMP

5. Absalom's forces attack David's forces in the forest of Ephraim.

FOREST OF EPHRAIM

Mahanaim?
DAVID'S CAMP

Jabbok River

AMMON

1. Absalom murders Amnon to avenge his sister's humiliation.

Aphek

Jordan River

Baal-hazor
Ephraim?

Rabbah

Gilgal?

Bahurim?
Jerusalem
En-rogel

6. People from Judah and Benjamin meet David at the Jordan River to welcome him back to Jerusalem.

PHILISTIA

Gath

Tekoa

Dead Sea

Hebron

4. Absalom stages a rebellion against David in Hebron.

3. A woman from Tekoa deceives David to reconcile him with Absalom.

Beersheba

MOAB

N

Copyright © 2007 by Barbour Publishing, Inc.

JERUSALEM DURING SOLOMON'S TIME

A place of great importance to many, the Temple Mount is considered a holy site by members of the Jewish, Christian, and Muslim faiths. Such strong interest often results in political and religious conflict. Currently, the Temple Mount is under Islamic control.

This photograph, taken from the east, shows some ancient walls—built sometime after Solomon—as they exist today. (These are also noted on the map). The walls pictured were more expansive than the walls and city of Solomon's day. During the time of Solomon's reign, the city was smaller and simpler, but was certainly an adequate hub for social, commercial, and religious activity in ancient Israel.

The temple and home of Solomon were known to be glorious structures. The description of their sizes and some of their ornamentation can be found in 1 Kings 5–8.

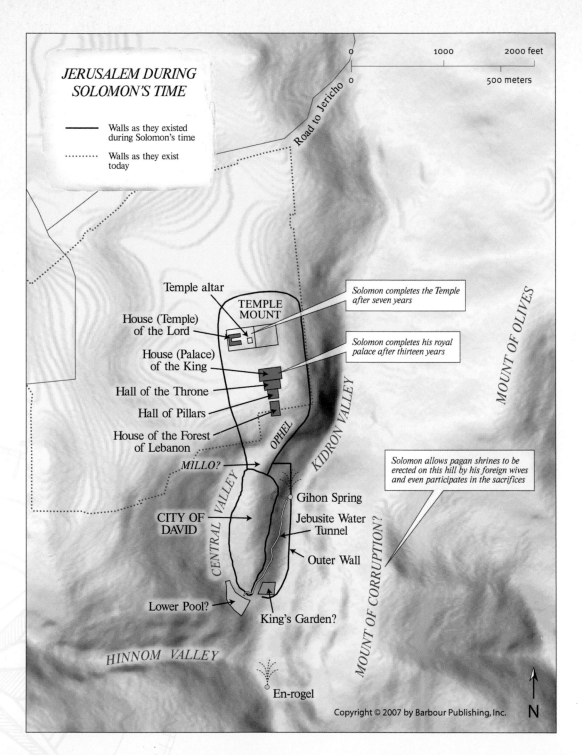

JERUSALEM DURING SOLOMON'S TIME

—— Walls as they existed during Solomon's time

········· Walls as they exist today

0   1000   2000 feet

0   500 meters

Road to Jericho

Temple altar

TEMPLE MOUNT

House (Temple) of the Lord

Solomon completes the Temple after seven years

House (Palace) of the King

Solomon completes his royal palace after thirteen years

Hall of the Throne

Hall of Pillars

House of the Forest of Lebanon

OPHEL

KIDRON VALLEY

MOUNT OF OLIVES

MILLO?

Solomon allows pagan shrines to be erected on this hill by his foreign wives and even participates in the sacrifices

Gihon Spring

CITY OF DAVID

CENTRAL VALLEY

Jebusite Water Tunnel

Outer Wall

MOUNT OF CORRUPTION?

Lower Pool?

King's Garden?

HINNOM VALLEY

En-rogel

N

Copyright © 2007 by Barbour Publishing, Inc.

SOLOMON'S ADMINISTRATIVE DISTRICTS

Solomon completed many great building projects throughout the land of Israel (see 1 Kings 5–7; 9:15–22 for more details). Solomon used slave labor to complete the work, though he never enslaved fellow Israelites. Rather, he appointed his fellow countrymen as soldiers, officials, commanders, and captains (1 Kings 9:22).

Solomon built ships to bring building supplies from northern lands to Jerusalem (see the blue lines on the map). The cedars of Lebanon (see photo) were highly prized in the ancient world, and Solomon used them generously when building the temple and royal palace.

In addition to massive building projects, Solomon built a civil infrastructure for ruling the people wisely and efficiently. (The administrative districts he created are located on the map and can be read about in 1 Kings 4.) During this time, Israel's economy prospered and the people flourished; "Judah and Israel were as numerous as the sand on the seashore; they ate, they drank and they were happy" (1 Kings 4:20).

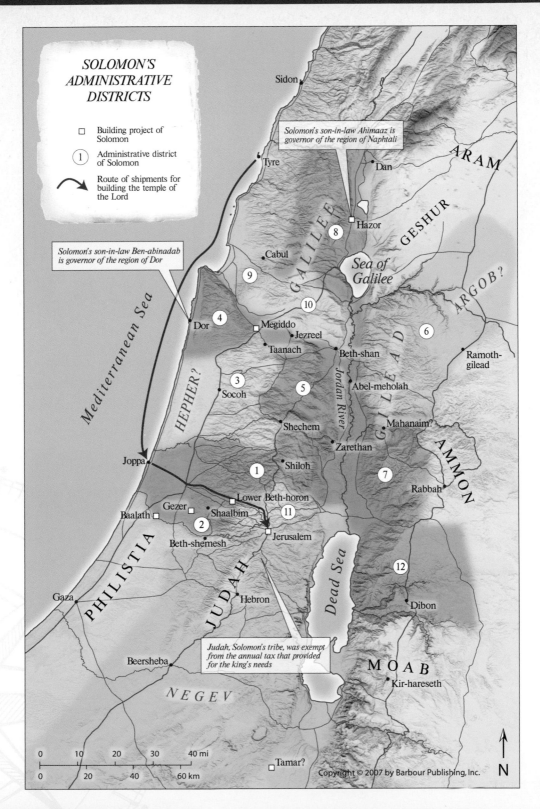

SOLOMON'S ADMINISTRATIVE DISTRICTS

☐ Building project of Solomon

① Administrative district of Solomon

→ Route of shipments for building the temple of the Lord

Solomon's son-in-law Ben-abinadab is governor of the region of Dor

Solomon's son-in-law Ahimaaz is governor of the region of Naphtali

Judah, Solomon's tribe, was exempt from the annual tax that provided for the king's needs

Sidon

Tyre

Dan

ARAM

GESHUR

Hazor

8

GALILEE

Cabul

Sea of Galilee

9

Dor

4

10

HEPHER?

Megiddo

Jezreel

Taanach

Beth-shan

ARGOB?

6

Ramoth-gilead

Mediterranean Sea

3

Socoh

5

Jordan River

Abel-meholah

GILEAD

Mahanaim?

Shechem

Zarethan

AMMON

1

Shiloh

7

Rabbah

Joppa

Lower Beth-horon

Gezer

Baalath

2

Shaalbim

11

Jerusalem

Beth-shemesh

12

JUDAH

PHILISTIA

Gaza

Hebron

Dead Sea

Dibon

Beersheba

MOAB

NEGEV

Kir-hareseth

0 10 20 30 40 mi

0 20 40 60 km

Tamar?

Copyright © 2007 by Barbour Publishing, Inc.

N

SOLOMON'S INTERNATIONAL VENTURES

In addition to bringing peace, security, and building projects to the Holy Land, Solomon also brought economic prosperity. In fact, he accumulated so much gold that silver had little value (1 Kings 10:27; 2 Chronicles 9:20).

One of the ways Solomon increased the wealth of the country was through increasing the import and export business. For example, he purchased horses from Kue and Egypt to sell to the Hittites and Arameans (1 Kings 10:29). In addition to trading with his neighbors, Solomon built merchant ships that expanded commerce. First Kings 9:26 records information about the fleet that Solomon built on the Red Sea, which also contributed to trade efforts (see lines in red). In addition to these, he had other ships that returned "every three years. . .carrying gold, silver and ivory, and apes and baboons" (2 Chronicles 9:21). Israel's economy also grew and prospered by virtue of the country's location. As a centrally located, peaceful land, Israel became a natural trade route for merchants from all surrounding countries.

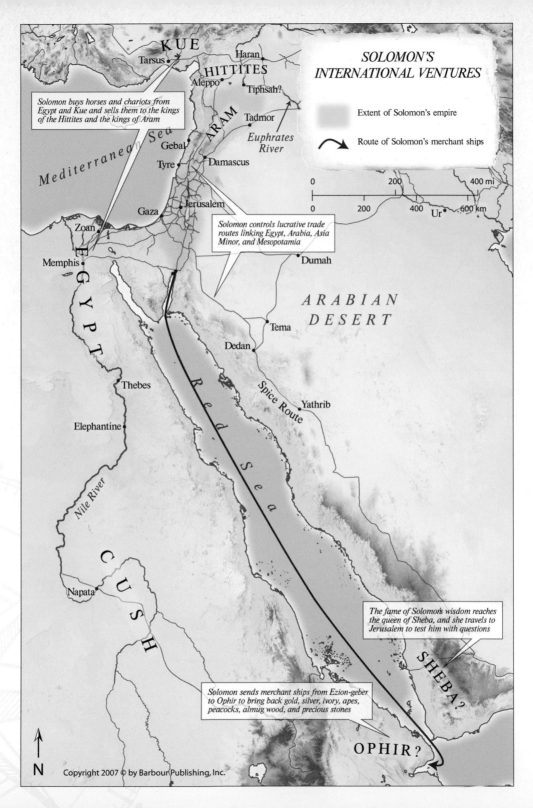

SOLOMON'S INTERNATIONAL VENTURES

Extent of Solomon's empire

Route of Solomon's merchant ships

KUE

Tarsus

HITTITES

Haran

Aleppo

Tiphsah?

ARAM

Tadmor

Euphrates River

Solomon buys horses and chariots from Egypt and Kue and sells them to the kings of the Hittites and the kings of Aram

Mediterranean Sea

Gebal

Tyre

Damascus

Gaza

Jerusalem

Zoan

Solomon controls lucrative trade routes linking Egypt, Arabia, Asia Minor, and Mesopotamia

Dumah

Memphis

EGYPT

Ur

ARABIAN DESERT

Tema

Dedan

Spice Route

Thebes

Yathrib

Elephantine

Red Sea

Nile River

CUSH

Napata

The fame of Solomon's wisdom reaches the queen of Sheba, and she travels to Jerusalem to test him with questions

SHEBA?

Solomon sends merchant ships from Ezion-geber to Ophir to bring back gold, silver, ivory, apes, peacocks, almug wood, and precious stones

OPHIR?

N

0   200   400 mi

0   200   400   600 km

THE KINGDOM DIVIDES

After Solomon's death, Israel divided into two kingdoms: the Northern Kingdom and the Southern Kingdom. The ten tribes of the north rebelled against King Rehoboam, seceded from the kingdom, and established Jeroboam as the king of the "new" Israel. In the south, the tribe of Judah remained loyal to King Rehoboam and the Davidic line and became known as the nation of Judah.

Since the Southern Kingdom controlled the temple, King Jeroboam of the Northern Kingdom feared his people would defect when they traveled to Jerusalem to worship: "Jeroboam thought to himself, 'The kingdom will now likely revert to the house of David. If these people go up to offer sacrifices at

the temple of the LORD in Jerusalem, they will again give their allegiance to their lord, Rehoboam king of Judah. They will kill me and return to King Rehoboam' " (1 Kings 12:26–27).

To avoid this end, King Jeroboam set up idols at Bethel and Dan (see map). These conveniently-located cities sat on the northern and southern ends of the kingdom and became centers of worship for the people living in the Northern Kingdom. The photograph shows the actual site of the high place in the northern city of Dan. The reconstructed metal frame shows the probable location and size of the original altar built by Jeroboam.

Soon after the kingdom divided, King Shishak of Egypt raided the cities of Judah and Israel, carrying off significant treasures and wealth. The biblical account includes references to the attacks against Judah's cities, and archaeological evidence reveals that the attacks also included some of Israel's northern cities (2 Chronicles 12).

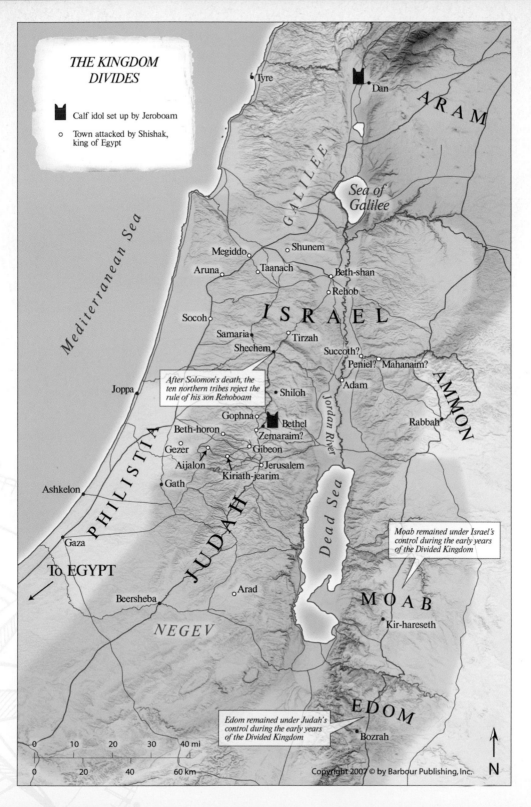

THE KINGDOM DIVIDES

■ Calf idol set up by Jeroboam

○ Town attacked by Shishak, king of Egypt

Tyre

Dan

A R A M

GALILEE

Sea of Galilee

Megiddo
Shunem
Aruna
Taanach
Beth-shan
Rehob

Socoh

I S R A E L

Samaria
Tirzah
Shechem
Succoth?
Peniel?
Mahanaim?
Adam

A M M O N

Mediterranean Sea

Joppa

After Solomon's death, the ten northern tribes reject the rule of his son Rehoboam

Shiloh

Jordan River

Gophna
Bethel
Beth-horon
Zemaraim?
Gezer
Gibeon
Aijalon
Jerusalem
Kiriath-jearim
Rabbah

P H I L I S T I A

Gath

Ashkelon

J U D A H

Gaza

Dead Sea

Moab remained under Israel's control during the early years of the Divided Kingdom

To EGYPT

Arad

Beersheba

M O A B

N E G E V

Kir-hareseth

E D O M

Edom remained under Judah's control during the early years of the Divided Kingdom

Bozrah

0	10	20	30	40 mi
0	20	40		60 km

N

Copyright 2007 © by Barbour Publishing, Inc.

ISRAEL'S WARS WITH ARAM

At war with King Baasha of the Northern Kingdom of Israel, King Asa of the Southern Kingdom of Judah refused to trust God for protection and instead made a treaty with Ben-Hadad (king of Damascus in Aram). The treaty effectively sandwiched the Northern Kingdom between two adversarial nations, causing the Northern Kingdom to end its siege on Judah.

During this period, Ben-hadad attacked and captured several cities in the Northern Kingdom, including the city of Dan (1 Kings 15:9–22).

Archaeologists have since reconstructed a portion of Dan's formidable fortifications (see photo).

Ben-hadad's son, Ben-hadad II, assembled a large army and led a series of attacks against the people of Israel (see lines on map). The blue line records a battle at Aphek where God fought for the Northern Kingdom (1 Kings 20). The red line recounts the battle for Samaria (2 Kings 6:24–33). The green line represents a battle between Aram and God's people (1 Kings 22); in this battle, Israel and Judah joined forces to repel the attacking Arameans, and King Ahab of Israel was killed by a "random" arrow shot into the battle.

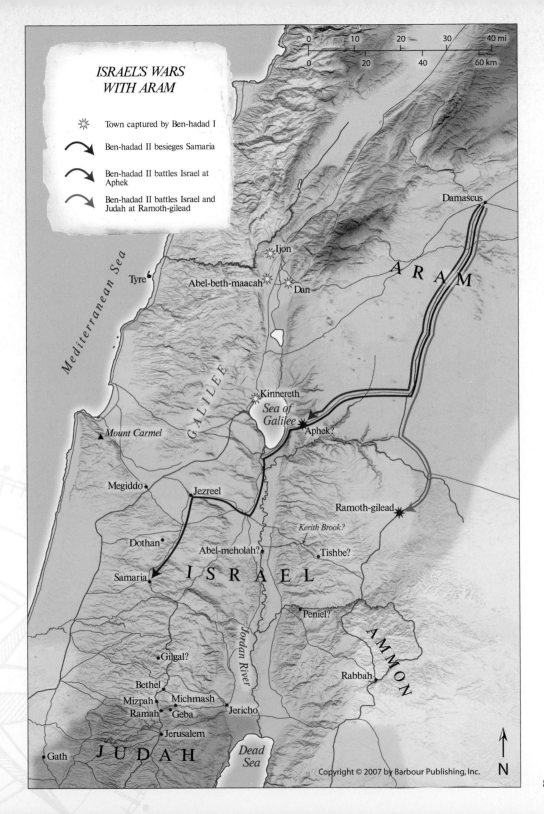

ISRAEL'S WARS WITH ARAM

✳ Town captured by Ben-hadad I

➤ Ben-hadad II besieges Samaria

➤ Ben-hadad II battles Israel at Aphek

➤ Ben-hadad II battles Israel and Judah at Ramoth-gilead

0   10   20   30   40 mi

0   20   40   60 km

Mediterranean Sea

Damascus

A R A M

Tyre

Ijon

Abel-beth-maacah   Dan

G A L I L E E

Kinnereth
Sea of Galilee
Aphek?

▲ Mount Carmel

Megiddo   Jezreel

Ramoth-gilead

Kerith Brook?

Dothan   Abel-meholah?   Tishbe?

Samaria   I S R A E L

Peniel?

Gilgal?   Jordan River   A M M O N

Bethel   Rabbah

Mizpah   Michmash
Ramah   Geba   Jericho

Jerusalem

Gath   J U D A H   Dead Sea

N

MOAB, EDOM, AND LIBNAH REVOLT

Within one hundred years of King Solomon's death, the reach and power of the Israelites began to wane. In a previous generation, a united kingdom had expanded its borders and ruled over neighboring nations. Now, with the kingdom divided and weakened, neighboring countries that had once paid tributes broke free and became hostile neighbors.

During the reign of Joram (also called Jehoram) of Israel, Moab stopped paying its yearly tribute of two hundred thousand animals. When they rebelled, King Joram allied with King Jehosaphat of Judah and together they attacked Kir-hareseth, the capital of Moab. While the city was well-situated and the rugged terrain gave it a good defense, the allied kings inflicted great casualties on the people of Moab (2 Kings 3). In the end, however, Moab still maintained its independence.

After Jehoshaphat's death, Jehoram became king of Judah. During his reign, Edom and their capital city of Bozrah (see photo) rebelled against the house of David, which still ruled Judah. In response, Jehoram mustered his army and traveled to the region of Edom. The Edomites won an initial strategic position and King Jehoram's army abandoned the cause and fled home. Thus, Edom secured its independence. Around the same time, the Levitical city of Libnah rebelled against Jehoram because of his disobedience to God's commands (2 Kings 8:22; 2 Chronicles 21:10).

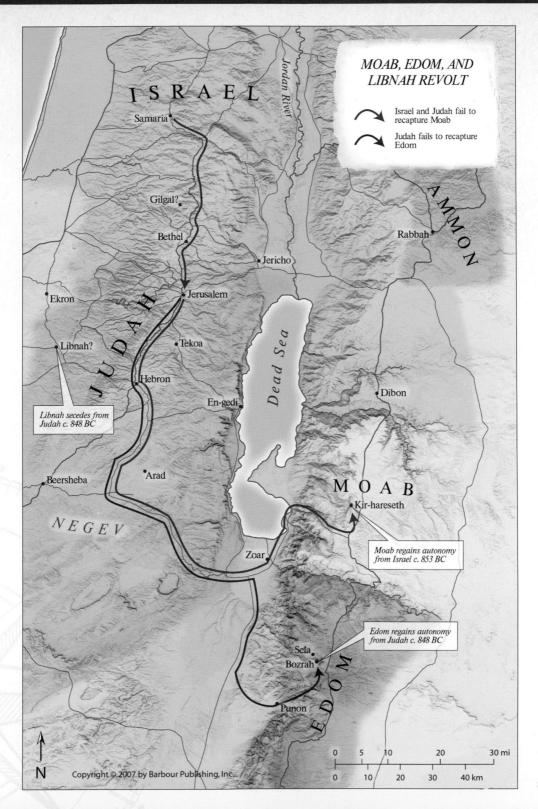

MOAB, EDOM, AND LIBNAH REVOLT

Israel and Judah fail to recapture Moab

Judah fails to recapture Edom

ISRAEL

Samaria

Gilgal?

Bethel

Jericho

Jerusalem

Ekron

Tekoa

Libnah?

Hebron

En-gedi

Libnah secedes from
Judah c. 848 BC

Beersheba

Arad

NEGEV

Zoar

Sela
Bozrah

Punon

Jordan River

AMMON

Rabbah

Dead Sea

Dibon

MOAB

Kir-hareseth

Moab regains autonomy
from Israel c. 853 BC

Edom regains autonomy
from Judah c. 848 BC

EDOM

JUDAH

0	5	10	20	30 mi

0	10	20	30	40 km

N

Copyright © 2007 by Barbour Publishing, Inc.

83

EVENTS DURING JEHU'S REIGN

Injured in battle against the Arameans, King Joram of Israel traveled to Jezreel to recover from his wounds. While Joram recuperated, the prophet Elisha anointed Jehu as the new king of Israel. Jehu rallied his men, left the battle in Ramoth Gilead, and conspired to take the kingdom from Joram.

Jehu secured his reign by killing Joram, mortally wounding King Ahaziah of Judah, killing Jezebel, and slaughtering the many members of Ahab's and Ahaziah's families. Without any remaining competitors, Jehu assumed the throne in Samaria.

While Jehu succeeded in securing his place as king, he was less effective in securing the borders of Israel; he lost all the land east of the Jordan to Hazael, king of Aram. This fertile land, settled at one time by the tribe of Manasseh because of its ability to house large flocks, became the property of Aram (see photo). Read the story of Jehu in 2 Kings 9–10.

In addition to the biblical account, archaeological evidence indicates that the king of Assyria exacted a heavy and humiliating tribute from Jehu.

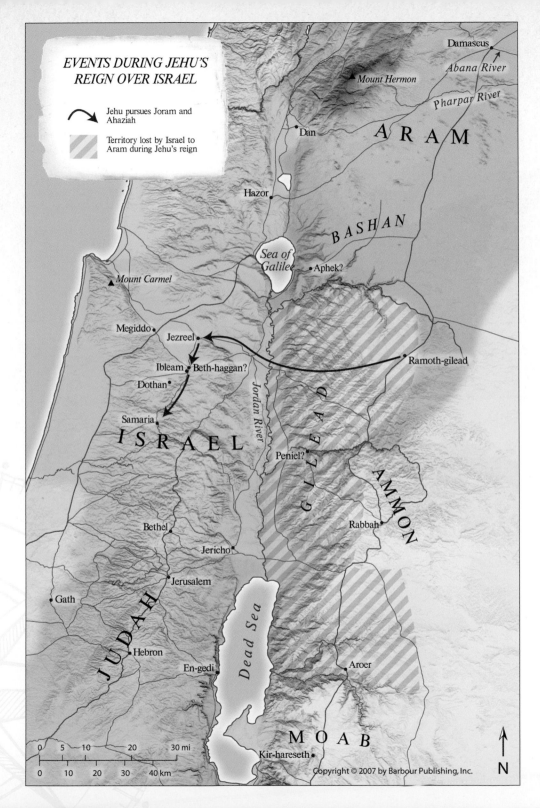

EVENTS DURING JEHU'S
REIGN OVER ISRAEL

Jehu pursues Joram and
Ahaziah

Territory lost by Israel to
Aram during Jehu's reign

Damascus

Abana River

Mount Hermon

Pharpar River

A R A M

Dan

BASHAN

Hazor

Sea of
Galilee

Aphek?

Mount Carmel

Megiddo

Jezreel

Ramoth-gilead

Ibleam   Beth-haggan?

Dothan

Jordan River

Samaria

I S R A E L

G I L E A D

Peniel?

AMMON

Bethel

Rabbah

Jericho

Jerusalem

Gath

J U D A H

Hebron

En-gedi

Dead Sea

Aroer

0   5   10   20   30 mi

0 10 20 30 40 km

M O A B

Kir-hareseth

Copyright © 2007 by Barbour Publishing, Inc.

N

85

RESURGENCE DURING THE REIGNS OF JEROBOAM II AND AZARIAH

Jeroboam II reigned forty-one years as king of the Northern Kingdom. Best known for his military accomplishments, he "restored the boundaries of Israel from Lebo Hamath to the Sea of the Arabah [the Dead Sea]... he recovered for Israel both Damascus and Hamath" (2 Kings 14:25, 28). Jeroboam reigned during a period of economic prosperity and was a contemporary of the prophets Hosea, Amos, and Jonah.

During the same time, Azariah (also called Uzziah) became king of the Southern Kingdom and reigned fifty-two years (see 2 Kings 15; 2 Chronicles 26). He also led his kingdom through a period of military and economic prosperity. He recaptured and rebuilt Elath, an important trading city on the Red Sea. He defeated the Philistine cities in the west (see photo for a view of this coastal region near Ashdod and Jabneh), the Arabs near Gurbaal, and the Meunites. "The Ammonites brought tribute to Uzziah, and his fame spread as far as the border of Egypt, because he had become very powerful" (2 Chronicles 26:8).

Unfortunately, his many successes gave him too much confidence, as 2 Chronicles 26:16 records: "But after Uzziah became powerful, his pride led to his downfall. He was unfaithful to the LORD his God, and entered the temple of the LORD to burn incense on the altar of incense." As a result of this sinful action, God struck Uzziah with leprosy and the king remained an outcast until he died.

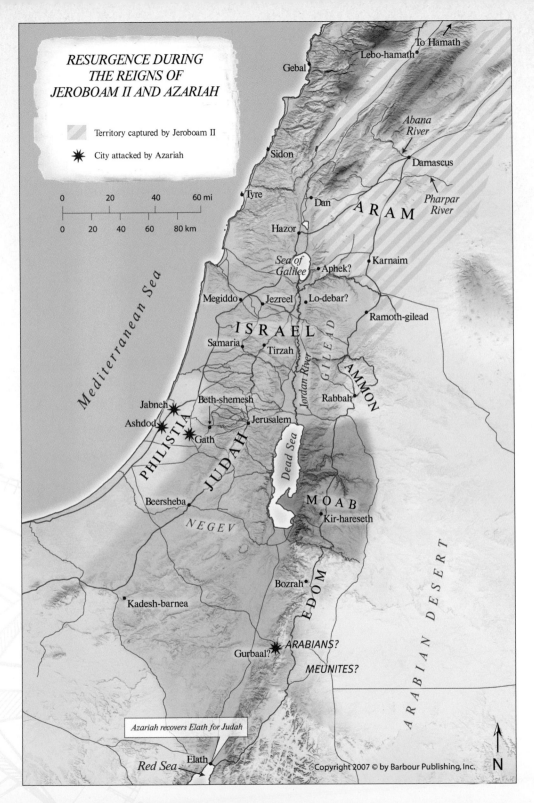

RESURGENCE DURING
THE REIGNS OF
JEROBOAM II AND AZARIAH

Territory captured by Jeroboam II

City attacked by Azariah

0   20   40   60 mi

0   20   40   60   80 km

To Hamath

Lebo-hamath

Gebal

Abana
River

Sidon

Damascus

A R A M

Pharpar
River

Tyre

Dan

Hazor

Karnaim

Sea of
Galilee

Aphek?

Megiddo

Jezreel

Lo-debar?

Ramoth-gilead

I S R A E L

Samaria

Tirzah

G I L E A D

AMMON

Jordan River

Rabbah

Mediterranean Sea

Jabneh

Beth-shemesh

Ashdod

Jerusalem

Gath

P H I L I S T I A

J U D A H

Dead Sea

M O A B

Beersheba

Kir-hareseth

N E G E V

Bozrah

EDOM

Kadesh-barnea

A R A B I A N   D E S E R T

Gurbaal?

ARABIANS?

MEUNITES?

Azariah recovers Elath for Judah

Red Sea

Elath

N

Copyright 2007 © by Barbour Publishing, Inc.

87

THE ASSYRIAN EMPIRE DURING 2 KINGS

Hoshea became the last king of Israel and reigned nine years before the Assyrian army conquered the Northern Kingdom. Assyria then deported the people of Israel and resettled the land with foreigners. The Bible clearly indicates that "all this took place because the Israelites had sinned against the LORD their God, who had brought them up out of Egypt" (2 Kings 17:7).

Here is a list of the kings of the Northern Kingdom before the Assyrian conquest:

Jeroboam I	1 Kings 11:26–40; 12–14; 2 Chronicles 10
Nadab	1 Kings 15:25–32
Baasha	1 Kings 15:33–16:7
Elah	1 Kings 16:8–14
Zimri	1 Kings 16:15–20
Tibni	1 Kings 16:21–22
Omri	1 Kings 16:15–28
Ahab	1 Kings 16–22; 2 Chronicles 18
Ahaziah	1 Kings 22:51–53; 2 Kings 1
Jehoram (Joram)	2 Kings 3, 9
Jehu	2 Kings 9–10
Jehoahaz	2 Kings 13:1–9
Jehoash	2 Kings 13:10–25
Jeroboam II	2 Kings 14:23–29
Zechariah	2 Kings 15:8–12
Shallum	2 Kings 15:10–16
Menahem	2 Kings 15:14–22
Pekahiah	2 Kings 15:22–26
Pekah	2 Kings 15:25–31
Hoshea	2 Kings 15:30; 17:1–6

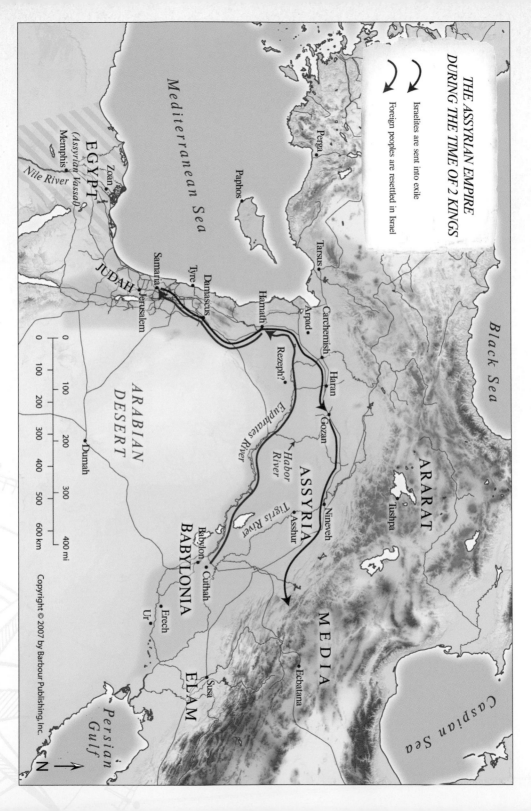

THE ASSYRIAN EMPIRE
DURING THE TIME OF 2 KINGS

Israelites are sent into exile

Foreign peoples are resettled in Israel

Mediterranean Sea

Black Sea

Caspian Sea

Persian Gulf

EGYPT
(Assyrian Vassal)

Memphis

Nile River

Zoan

Paphos

Perga

Tarsus

JUDAH

Samaria

Tyre

Damascus

Jerusalem

Hamath

Arpad

Carchemish

Rezeph?

Haran

Gozan

ARARAT

Tushpa

ARABIAN
DESERT

Euphrates River

Habor River

ASSYRIA

Nineveh

Asshur

Dumah

Tigris River

BABYLONIA

Babylon

Cuthah

Ur

Erech

ELAM

Susa

Ecbatana

MEDIA

0   100   200   300   400   500   600 km

0   100   200   300   400 mi

Copyright © 2007 by Barbour Publishing, Inc.

N

89

JERUSALEM DURING HEZEKIAH'S TIME

With the Northern Kingdom defeated and the people dispersed, the king of Assyria began also to threaten Judah with the same fate. In a dramatic confrontation that took place near the Upper Pool (see map), the people of Judah listened from the city wall and heard the taunts and threats of the Assyrian field commander, which he delivered to the king's officials in Hebrew.

Hezekiah responded to the Assyrian's challenge by praying to God. God answered his prayers with an encouraging prophecy from Isaiah. Soon afterward, an angel of the Lord struck the Assyrian camp, killing 185,000 soldiers, and King Sennacherib withdrew. (Read this story in 2 Kings 18–19. This event is also attested to by the ancient historian Herodotus.)

While the stories of his conquests, faith, and prayers have encouraged people throughout the centuries, Hezekiah also left behind one other lasting legacy. Second Kings 20:20 briefly mentions a water system created by Hezekiah. In 1838, western explorers discovered the 1,750 foot tunnel, which is considered one of the greatest feats of water engineering in the ancient world (see photo).

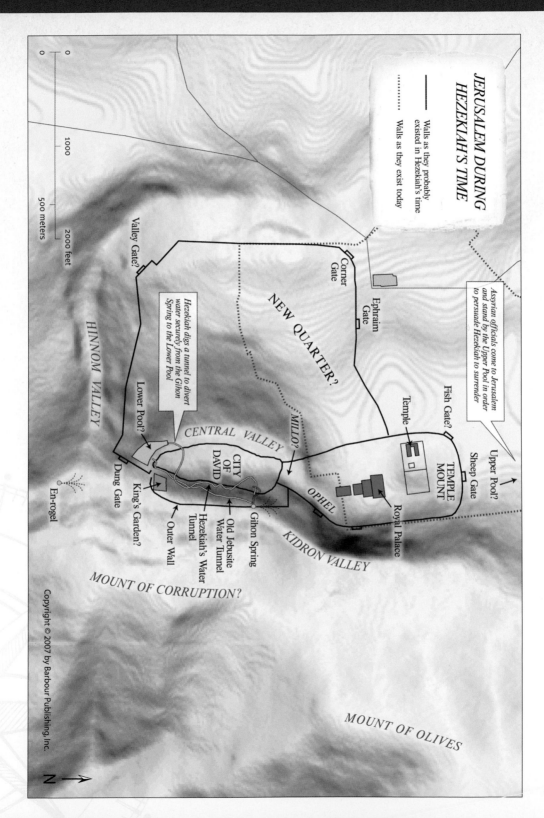

JERUSALEM DURING HEZEKIAH'S TIME

Walls as they probably existed in Hezekiah's time

Walls as they exist today

Assyrian officials come to Jerusalem and stand by the Upper Pool in order to persuade Hezekiah to surrender

Hezekiah digs a tunnel to divert water securely from the Gihon Spring to the Lower Pool

Corner Gate

Ephraim Gate

Valley Gate?

NEW QUARTER?

HINNOM VALLEY

Temple

Fish Gate?

Upper Pool?

Sheep Gate

TEMPLE MOUNT

MILLO?

Lower Pool?

CENTRAL VALLEY

CITY OF DAVID

OPHEL

Royal Palace

Dung Gate

King's Garden?

Hezekiah's Water Tunnel

Old Jebusite Water Tunnel

Gihon Spring

En-rogel

Outer Wall

KIDRON VALLEY

MOUNT OF CORRUPTION?

MOUNT OF OLIVES

N →

0   0
1000   500 meters
2000 feet

Copyright © 2007 by Barbour Publishing, Inc.

91

EVENTS DURING JOSIAH'S REIGN OVER JUDAH

Although Assyria was the greatest military power in the region, it received growing pressure from Babylon. When the two powers began to engage in hostilities, the Assyrians called upon the king of Egypt, their vassal, to help defeat their enemies.

King Neco of Egypt quickly moved his armies along the most direct route to the battle, which took him through Josiah's Judah. Josiah mobilized for battle and opposed the Egyptians at Megiddo, where he was defeated and killed. King Neco continued to Carchemish but was himself met with defeat by Nebuchadnezzar's Babylonian army—the new, undisputed military power in the region. This photo shows arrowheads from the great battle at Carchemish, on display at the British Museum.

Despite his ill-fated decision to battle the Egyptians, Josiah was regarded as a good and effective king. He expanded the borders of the country, rid the land of idolatry, and worked at renewing the monotheistic religious practices of the people of Judah. Read his story in 2 Kings 22:1–23:30 and 2 Chronicles 34–35.

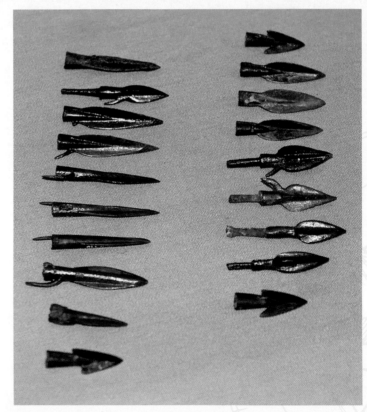

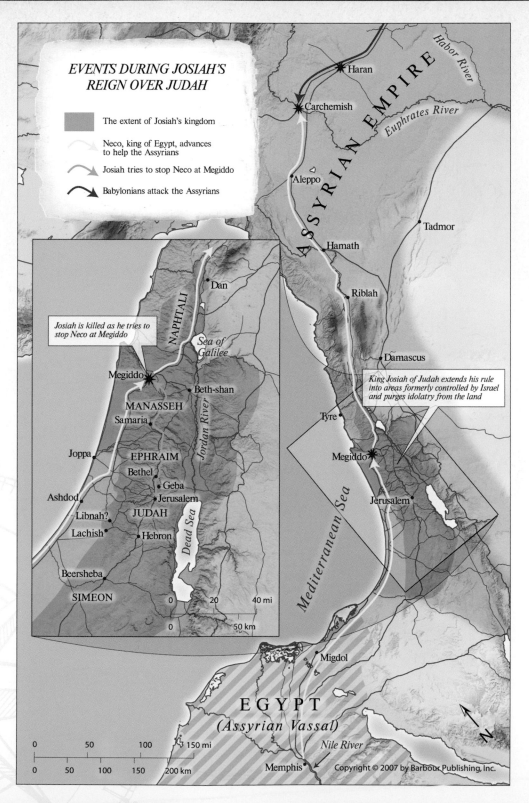

EVENTS DURING JOSIAH'S REIGN OVER JUDAH

- The extent of Josiah's kingdom
- Neco, king of Egypt, advances to help the Assyrians
- Josiah tries to stop Neco at Megiddo
- Babylonians attack the Assyrians

Josiah is killed as he tries to stop Neco at Megiddo

King Josiah of Judah extends his rule into areas formerly controlled by Israel and purges idolatry from the land

Haran

Carchemish

Habor River

ASSYRIAN EMPIRE

Euphrates River

Aleppo

Tadmor

Hamath

Riblah

Damascus

Tyre

Megiddo

Jerusalem

Mediterranean Sea

Dan

Sea of Galilee

NAPHTALI

Megiddo

Beth-shan

MANASSEH

Samaria

Jordan River

Joppa

EPHRAIM

Bethel

Geba

Jerusalem

Ashdod

Libnah?

JUDAH

Lachish

Hebron

Dead Sea

Beersheba

SIMEON

0   20   40 mi

0   50 km

Migdol

E G Y P T
(Assyrian Vassal)

Nile River

Memphis

N

0   50   100   150 mi

0   50   100   150   200 km

Copyright © 2007 by Barbour Publishing, Inc.

THE BABYLONIAN EMPIRE DURING 2 KINGS

Though the southern kingdom of Judah outlasted the Northern Kingdom, it eventually fell to the Babylonian Empire and its people were sent into exile. Unlike most of their brothers to the north, many citizens of the Southern Kingdom eventually returned to the promised land. Below is a list of kings (and one queen) who ruled the Southern Kingdom of Judah before the people were exiled.

Rehoboam	1 Kings 12:1–24; 14:21–31; 2 Chronicles 10–12
Abijah	1 Kings 15:1–8; 2 Chronicles 13
Asa	1 Kings 15:9–24; 2 Chronicles 14–16
Jehoshaphat	1 Kings 22; 2 Chronicles 17–20
Joram (Jehoram)	2 Kings 8:16–24; 2 Chronicles 21
Ahaziah	2 Kings 8:25–29; 2 Chronicles 22:1–9
Queen Athaliah	2 Kings 11; 2 Chronicles 22:10–23:21
Joash	2 Kings 12; 2 Chronicles 24
Amaziah	2 Kings 14:1–22; 2 Chronicles 25
Azariah (Uzziah)	2 Kings 15:1–7; 2 Chronicles 26
Jotham	2 Kings 15:32–38; 2 Chronicles 27
Ahaz	2 Kings 16; 2 Chronicles 28
Hezekiah	2 Kings 18–20; 2 Chronicles 29–32; Isaiah 36–39
Manasseh	2 Kings 21:1–18; 2 Chronicles 33:1–20
Amon	2 Kings 21:19–26; 2 Chronicles 33:21–25
Josiah	2 Kings 22:1–23:30; 2 Chronicles 34–35
Jehoahaz	2 Kings 23:31–35; 2 Chronicles 36:1–4
Jehoiakim	2 Kings 23:36–24:6; 2 Chronicles 36:5–8
Jehoiachin	2 Kings 24:8–17, 25:27–30; 2 Chronicles 36:9–10
Zedekiah	2 Kings 24:18–25:7; 2 Chronicles 36:11–14

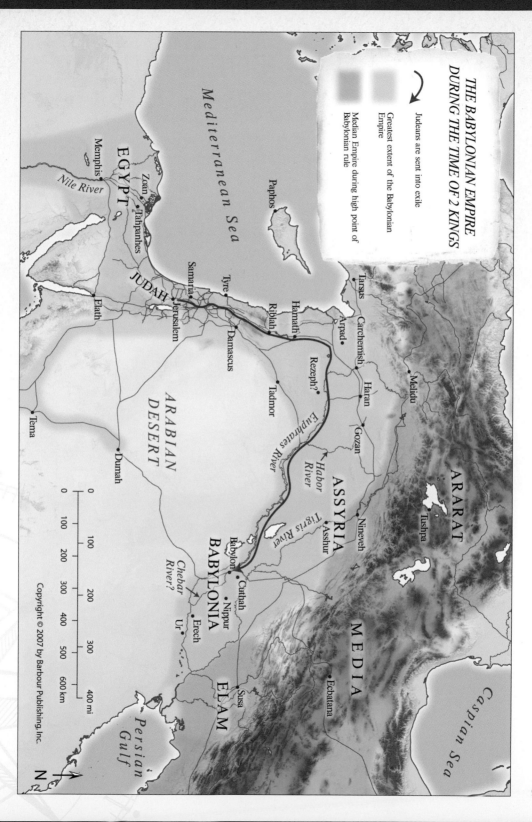

THE BABYLONIAN EMPIRE
DURING THE TIME OF 2 KINGS

Judeans are sent into exile

Greatest extent of the Babylonian Empire

Median Empire during high point of Babylonian rule

Mediterranean Sea

EGYPT
Memphis
Nile River
Zoan
Tahpanhes
Elath

Paphos

JUDAH
Samaria
Tyre
Jerusalem
Damascus
Hamath
Riblah
Rezeph?
Tadmor

Tarsus
Arpad
Carchemish
Haran
Gozan
Melidu

Euphrates River
Habor River
ASSYRIA
Nineveh
Asshur
Tigris River

ARARAT
Tushpa

ARABIAN
DESERT
Tema
Dumah

BABYLONIA
Babylon
Chebar River?
Cuthah
Nippur
Erech
Ur

MEDIA
Ecbatana

ELAM
Susa

Caspian Sea

Persian Gulf

N

0   100   200   300   400   500   600 km
0   100   200   300   400 mi

Copyright © 2007 by Barbour Publishing, Inc.

95

ISRAEL DURING THE TIME OF 1 CHRONICLES

Below are key events in the history of the Hebrew monarchy:	
1051 BC	Saul becomes the first king of Israel.
1011 BC	David becomes king of Judah.
960 BC	The first temple is built in Jerusalem, replacing the tabernacle built by Moses (see photos of reconstruction of Tabernacle).
930 BC	The kingdom divides into two countries. The northern is known as Israel, and the southern is known as Judah.
722 BC	The ten tribes of the Northern Kingdom are conquered by Assyria and driven into exile. These tribes never return.
586 BC	The southern kingdom of Judah falls to Babylon.

The biblical timeline continues on page 106.

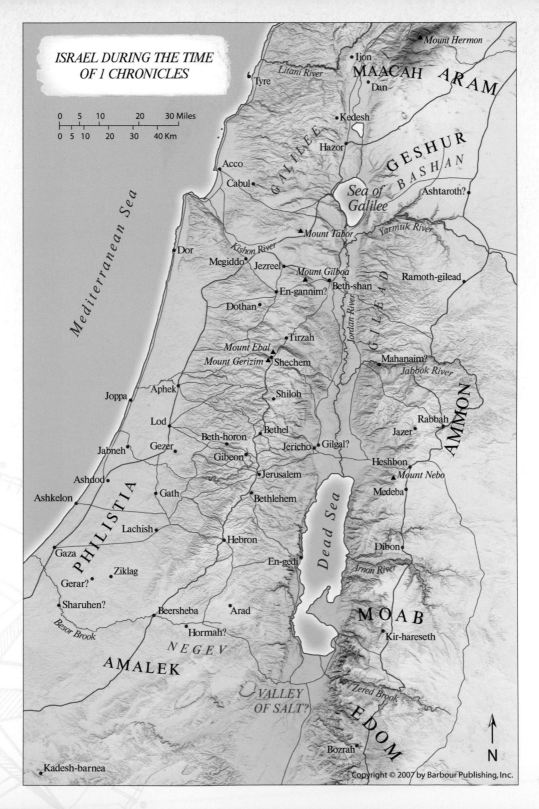

ISRAEL DURING THE TIME OF 1 CHRONICLES

0   5   10   20   30 Miles

0 5 10   20   30   40 Km

Mount Hermon

Ijon

Tyre

Litani River

MAACAH

ARAM

Dan

Kedesh

GALILEE

Hazor

GESHUR

BASHAN

Acco

Cabul

Sea of Galilee

Ashtaroth?

Mediterranean Sea

Dor

Mount Tabor

Yarmuk River

Megiddo

Kishon River

Jezreel

Ramoth-gilead

Mount Gilboa

En-gannim?

Beth-shan

GILEAD

Dothan

Jordan River

Tirzah

Mount Ebal

Mahanaim?

Mount Gerizim

Shechem

Jabbok River

Aphek

Shiloh

Joppa

Lod

Bethel

Rabbah

AMMON

Beth-horon

Jericho

Jazer

Jabneh

Gezer

Gibeon

Gilgal?

Ashdod

Jerusalem

Heshbon

Mount Nebo

Gath

Bethlehem

Medeba

Ashkelon

PHILISTIA

Lachish

Dead Sea

Hebron

Dibon

Gaza

En-gedi

Ziklag

Arnon River

Gerar?

Sharuhen?

Beersheba

Arad

MOAB

Hormah?

NEGEV

Kir-hareseth

AMALEK

Zered Brook

Besor Brook

VALLEY OF SALT?

EDOM

Bozrah

N

Kadesh-barnea

EVENTS DURING ASA'S REIGN

During the rule of Asa, the Ethiopians attacked Judah. Coming from the south, Zerah led a sizeable army of the Ethiopians (also called the Cushites) into the southern portion of Judah.

In response, Asa mustered his own army, numbering 300,000 men, to battle the Ethiopians near Mareshah. Asa's army defeated his enemies, drove them back to Gerar, and eventually annihilated them. During the battle, Asa's armies also conquered the cities near Gerar, carrying off a substantial amount of plunder. Despite the fact that this region was in the dry Negev, it received enough rainfall to produce a plentiful harvest of fruits, grains, and vegetables (see photo of Gerar)—creating great wealth that became the property of Asa and his men. "They destroyed all the villages around Gerar, for the terror of the Lord had fallen upon them. They plundered all these villages, since there was much booty there. They also attacked the camps of the herdsmen and carried off droves of sheep and goats and camels. Then they returned to Jerusalem" (2 Chronicles 14:14–15).

Read the entire story in 2 Chronicles 14.

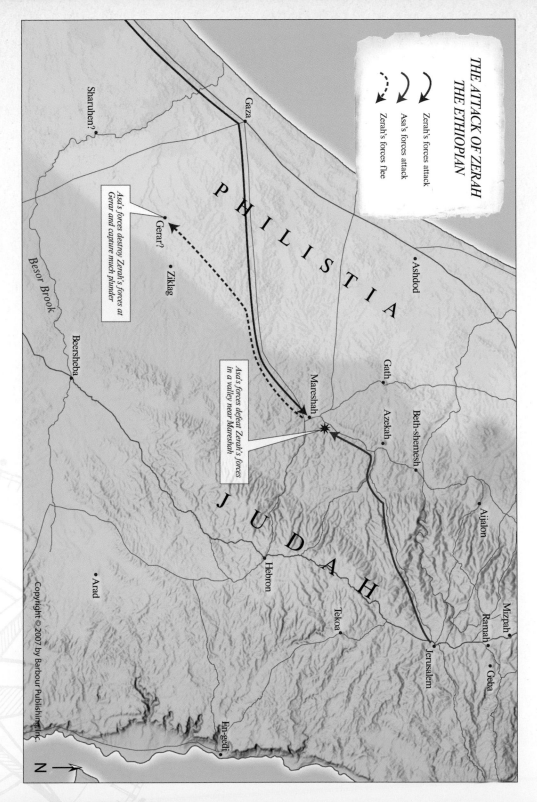

THE ATTACK OF ZERAH
THE ETHIOPIAN

Zerah's forces attack

Asa's forces attack

Zerah's forces flee

Sharuhen?

Gaza

P H I L I S T I A

Ashdod

Gerar?

Asa's forces destroy Zerah's forces at
Gerar and capture much plunder

Besor Brook

Ziklag

Beersheba

Mareshah

Asa's forces defeat Zerah's forces
in a valley near Mareshah

Gath

Azekah

Beth-shemesh

Ajalon

J U D A H

Arad

Hebron

Tekoa

Mizpah

Ramah

Geba

Jerusalem

En-gedi

N →

EVENTS DURING JEHOSHAPHAT'S REIGN OVER JUDAH

Though it regards Jehoshaphat as a good king, the biblical account of his reign reveals a man with a flawed record of devotion to God.

On the positive side, the biblical writers commend Jehoshaphat for his faith in God during a battle with the Moabites. When his enemies assembled a coalition of countries to fight against him, Jehoshaphat rallied the people to pray for God's help. God intervened by defeating the enemy while the army of Judah simply stood by and watched. While Jehoshaphat's soldiers awaited the battle, the enemy coalition fell apart as the allied countries began attacking each other rather than the Judeans (2 Chronicles 20:23).

On the negative side, the biblical accounts condemn Jehoshaphat for the alliance he made with King Ahaziah of the Northern Kingdom. Though this partnership must have seemed expedient, God did not approve of the alliance. God disciplined Jehoshaphat by destroying his merchant ships and long-term trading plans for Ezion-geber. A large storm likely blew up on the Red Sea (see photo) and destroyed the ships being built. While it might be easy to ascribe the cause of this event to merely natural phenomena, we learn in 1 Kings 22:48 and 2 Chronicles 20:37 that this was clearly an act of divine judgment.

Shortly after Jehoshaphat's death, his son Jehoram became king. Around this time, Moab rebelled from Israel, and Edom and Libnah revolted from Judah.

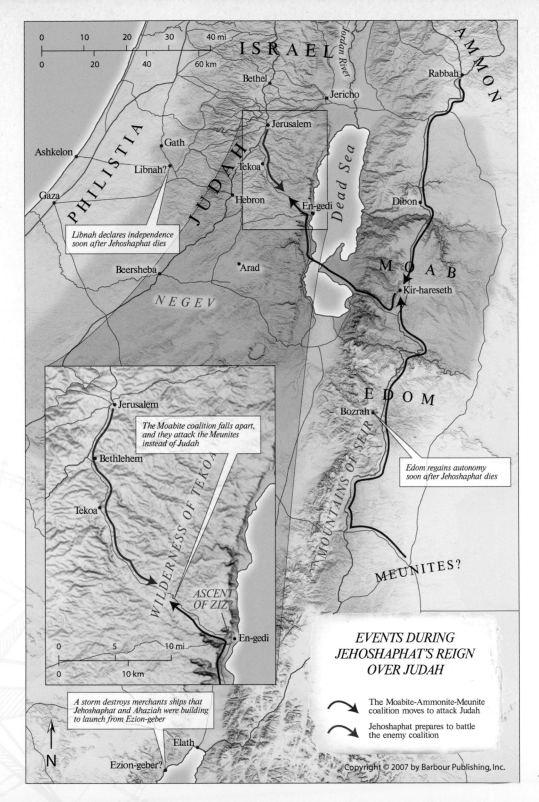

ISRAEL

0 10 20 30 40 mi

0 20 40 60 km

Bethel

Jordan River

Jericho

Jerusalem

AMMON

Rabbah

PHILISTIA

Gath

Ashkelon

Libnah?

JUDAH

Tekoa

Gaza

Hebron

En-gedi

Dead Sea

Dibon

Libnah declares independence
soon after Jehoshaphat dies

Beersheba

Arad

MOAB

Kir-hareseth

NEGEV

EDOM

Bozrah

MOUNTAINS OF SEIR

Jerusalem

The Moabite coalition falls apart,
and they attack the Meunites
instead of Judah

Edom regains autonomy
soon after Jehoshaphat dies

Bethlehem

WILDERNESS OF TEKOA

Tekoa

ASCENT
OF ZIZ?

0 5 10 mi

0 10 km

En-gedi

MEUNITES?

A storm destroys merchants ships that
Jehoshaphat and Ahaziah were building
to launch from Ezion-geber

N

Elath

Ezion-geber?

EVENTS DURING
JEHOSHAPHAT'S REIGN
OVER JUDAH

The Moabite-Ammonite-Meunite
coalition moves to attack Judah

Jehoshaphat prepares to battle
the enemy coalition

ARAM AND ISRAEL ATTACK JUDAH

Though not particularly well-known, Ahaz was certainly one of the most influential kings in Judah's history.

Spiritually, the biblical writers described Ahaz as an evil king who went as far as sacrificing his own son to pagan gods. As Ahaz faced attacks from all sides, the Bible says, "The LORD had humbled Judah because of Ahaz king of Israel, for he had promoted wickedness in Judah and had been most unfaithful to the LORD" (2 Chronicles 28:19). Toward the end of his reign, he closed the temple and set up altars to other gods throughout the land.

Militarily, the country of Judah was squeezed. While the Philistines captured cities in western Judah, Israel put pressure on them from the north. At the same time, Aram also attacked. Judah faced high casualty losses; in one battle with Israel the Judeans lost 120,000 men in the span of just one day.

Desperate, Ahaz sent for help from Assyria. The Assyrians arrived and defeated the invading armies, but they exacted a high cost for their help. Four long-term consequences resulted from Ahaz's actions:

1. Assyria stripped Judah of many financial resources.
2. The treasured city of Elath, known for its important trading port (see photo), was lost.
3. Assyria grew more powerful in the region.
4. By coming to the rescue of Judah, Assyria decimated the northern kingdom of Israel—eventually ending its very existence a few years later.

Read the full story in 2 Kings 16, 2 Chronicles 28, and Isaiah 7.

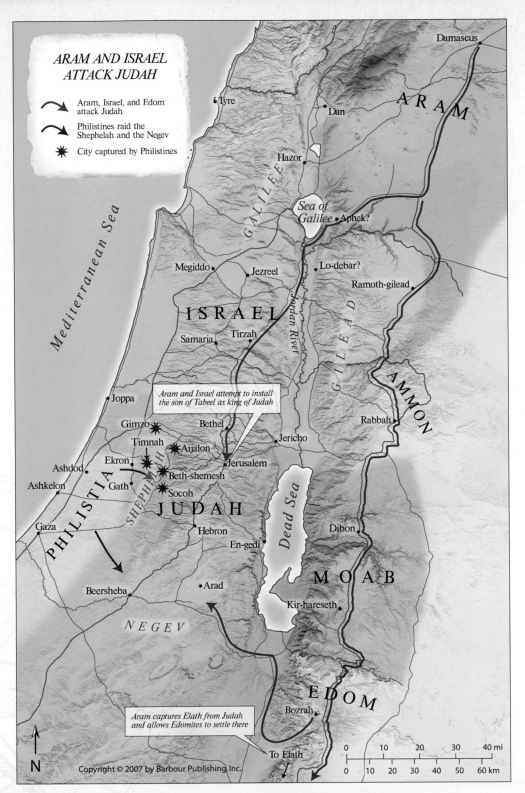

ARAM AND ISRAEL
ATTACK JUDAH

Aram, Israel, and Edom
attack Judah

Philistines raid the
Shephelah and the Negev

City captured by Philistines

Damascus

Tyre

Dan

A R A M

Hazor

GALILEE

Mediterranean Sea

Sea of
Galilee • Aphek?

Megiddo

Jezreel

Lo-debar?

Ramoth-gilead

I S R A E L

Jordan River

G I L E A D

Samaria

Tirzah

Joppa

Aram and Israel attempt to install
the son of Tabeel as king of Judah

Gimzo

Bethel

AMMON

Timnah

Aijalon

Jericho

Rabbah

Ekron

Jerusalem

Ashdod

SHEPHELAH

Beth-shemesh

Ashkelon

Gath

Socoh

J U D A H

Gaza

Hebron

Dead Sea

Dibon

PHILISTIA

En-gedi

Beersheba

Arad

M O A B

N E G E V

Kir-hareseth

E D O M

Aram captures Elath from Judah
and allows Edomites to settle there

Bozrah

To Elath

| 0 | 10 | 20 | 30 | 40 mi |

| 0 | 10 | 20 | 30 | 40 | 50 | 60 km |

N

Copyright © 2007 by Barbour Publishing, Inc.

EZRA LEADS EXILES BACK TO JUDEA

Although the Southern Kingdom had fallen and the people were taken away into captivity, God eventually brought them back to Judah (now called Judea), and the king of Persia commissioned a group of Jewish people to begin temple reconstruction. This account was consistent with the Persian practice of encouraging local worship within the regions they ruled. The Persian kings had preserved the treasures of the Hebrew temple and were ready to restore those treasures to the rebuilt temple.

Zerubbabel led the initial group of exiles back to Jerusalem. They began construction on the temple—laying the foundation in an emotional ceremony (Ezra 3:13). Work continued intermittently because of local pressures and opposition.

When the temple was finally completed, Ezra, a priest, led another group of Jewish people back to Jerusalem. With letters of endorsement and treasures from the king, Ezra returned to Jerusalem. With a deep understanding of and respect for the Law of Moses, Ezra helped the people restore proper Jewish practices.

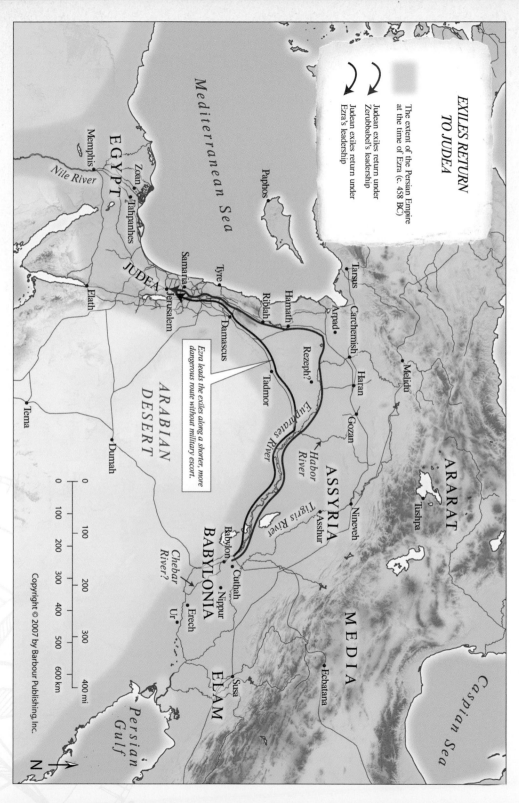

EXILES RETURN
TO JUDEA

The extent of the Persian Empire
at the time of Ezra (c. 458 BC)

Judean exiles return under
Zerubbabel's leadership

Judean exiles return under
Ezra's leadership

*Ezra leads the exiles along a shorter, more
dangerous route without military escort.*

Mediterranean Sea

Nile River

EGYPT

Memphis

Zoan
Tahpanhes

Elath

Tema

Dumah

JUDEA
Jerusalem

Samaria

Tyre

Damascus

Tadmor

Riblah

Hamath

Arpad

Paphos

Tarsus

Carchemish

Haran

Melitu

Rezeph?

Euphrates River

Gozan

*Habor
River*

ARABIAN
DESERT

ASSYRIA

Asshur

Nineveh

Tigris River

Babylon

Cuthah

Nippur

Erech

Ur

Chebar
River?

BABYLONIA

ELAM

Susa

Ecbatana

MEDIA

ARARAT

Tushpa

Caspian Sea

*Persian
Gulf*

N

0   100   200   300   400   500   600 km
0   100   200   300   400 mi

JUDEA DURING NEHEMIAH'S TIME

A cover-to-cover reading of the Bible doesn't yield all the information needed to understand the historical context of every book. The chart below chronologically portrays the order of events surrounding the Jewish exile. While many scholars disagree about the exact date and year of each event, the general flow of events is not usually challenged.

Key events between the exile of the Southern Kingdom and the work of Nehemiah	
586 BC	Nebuchadnezzar destroys Jerusalem and the temple. The Jewish people are deported to Babylon. Daniel serves as advisor to the kings of Babylon (and later of the Medes and Persians).
554 BC	Belshazzar begins to reign in Babylon.
539 BC	Cyrus the Mede conquers Babylon and sets up Darius as regional king. Daniel and the Jewish exiles are now subjects in the empire of the Medes and Persians.
538 BC	Zerubbabel brings a contingent of exiled Jewish people back to Israel. Temple reconstruction begins soon after.
520 BC	Zechariah and Haggai prophesy.
516 BC	The temple reconstruction is completed.
486 BC	Xerxes becomes king of Persia.
478 BC	Esther becomes queen of Persia.
464 BC	Artaxerxes assumes the throne in Persia.
458 BC	Ezra leads additional exiled Jews back to Judea.
445 BC	Nehemiah is commissioned to rebuild the walls.
425 BC	Malachi prophesies.

The biblical timeline continues on page 146.

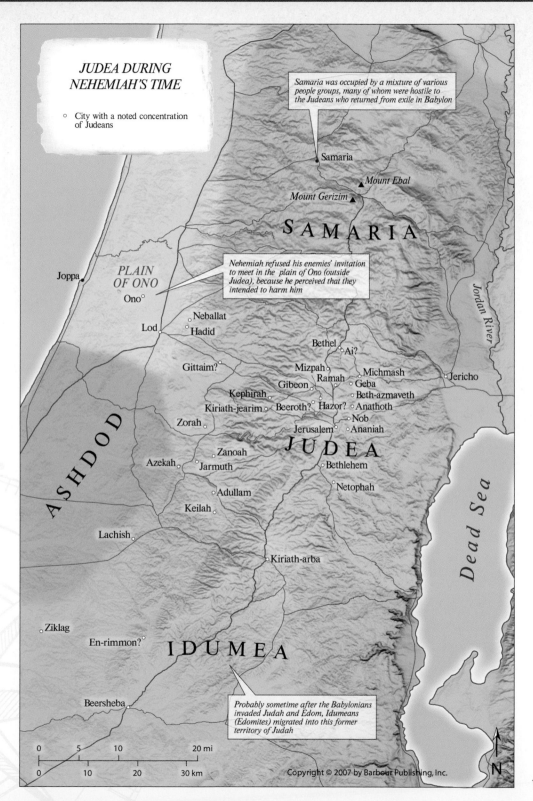

JUDEA DURING NEHEMIAH'S TIME

○ City with a noted concentration of Judeans

Samaria was occupied by a mixture of various people groups, many of whom were hostile to the Judeans who returned from exile in Babylon

Samaria

▲ Mount Ebal

Mount Gerizim ▲

SAMARIA

Joppa

PLAIN OF ONO

Nehemiah refused his enemies' invitation to meet in the plain of Ono (outside Judea), because he perceived that they intended to harm him

Ono ○

Jordan River

Neballat ○
Lod ○   ○ Hadid

Bethel ○ ○ Ai?

Gittaim? ○

Mizpah ○   Michmash ○
Ramah ○   ○ Geba
Gibeon ○   ○ Beth-azmaveth
Kephirah ○   Hazor? ○ Anathoth
Kiriath-jearim ○ Beeroth? ○   ○ Nob
Zorah ○   Jerusalem ○ ○ Ananiah

Jericho ○

JUDEA

Zanoah ○
Azekah ○ ○ Jarmuth   Bethlehem ○

○ Netophah

Adullam ○

Keilah ○

Lachish ○

Kiriath-arba ○

Dead Sea

Ziklag ○

En-rimmon? ○   **IDUMEA**

Probably sometime after the Babylonians invaded Judah and Edom, Idumeans (Edomites) migrated into this former territory of Judah

Beersheba ○

0	5	10		20 mi
0	10	20	30 km	

ASHDOD

Copyright © 2007 by Barbour Publishing, Inc.

N

NEHEMIAH REBUILDS JERUSALEM'S WALLS

Though glad to have the temple completed, the people of Jerusalem found themselves in a vulnerable position with the city walls still in ruins. Nehemiah, a Jew serving in Artaxerxes' court, petitioned the king—who granted his request—to lead a contingent back to Jerusalem to rebuild the city walls. The king gave Nehemiah letters guaranteeing his protection and providing the necessary supplies.

Nehemiah motivated the people to begin the effort of rebuilding the walls. When local troublemakers opposed them, the workers continued their task wearing swords in order to fend off their antagonists. Working nonstop, they completed the walls in a remarkably short time. The book of Nehemiah records that "the wall was completed. . .in fifty-two days. When all our enemies heard about this, all the surrounding nations were afraid and lost their self-confidence, because they realized that this work had been done with the help of our God" (Nehemiah 6:15–16).

With the wall completed, the people rededicated themselves to their faith in God as Ezra the priest read the Torah to the people. After the people had dedicated themselves, they also dedicated the walls of Jerusalem. This included having two choirs of Levites march along the city walls giving thanks to God (Nehemiah 12:27–47).

The tower on the right side of the photograph is believed to be remaining from the time of Nehemiah.

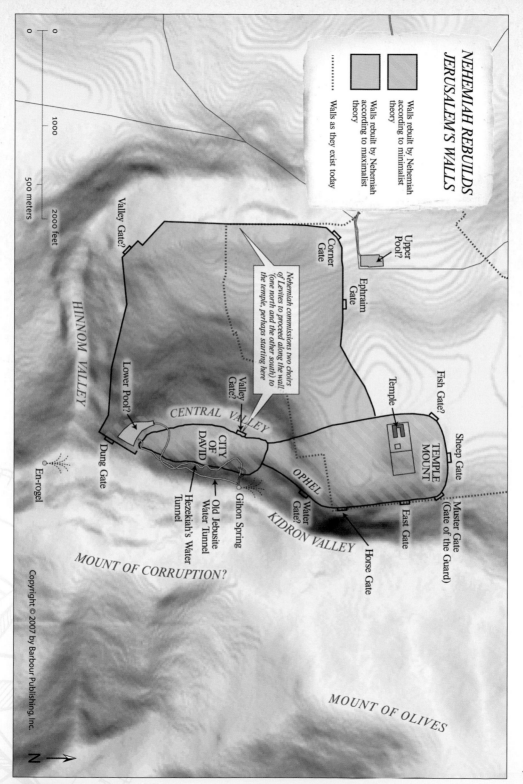

NEHEMIAH REBUILDS JERUSALEM'S WALLS

Walls rebuilt by Nehemiah according to minimalist theory

Walls rebuilt by Nehemiah according to maximalist theory

Walls as they exist today

Nehemiah commissions two choirs of Levites to proceed along the wall (one north and the other south) to the temple, perhaps starting here

Upper Pool?

Corner Gate

Ephraim Gate

Valley Gate?

Temple

Fish Gate?

Sheep Gate

Muster Gate (Gate of the Guard)

TEMPLE MOUNT

HINNOM VALLEY

CENTRAL VALLEY

Valley Gate?

Lower Pool?

CITY OF DAVID

OPHEL

Dung Gate

En-rogel

Hezekiah's Water Tunnel

Old Jebusite Water Tunnel

Gihon Spring

Water Gate?

East Gate

Horse Gate

KIDRON VALLEY

MOUNT OF CORRUPTION?

MOUNT OF OLIVES

0

0

1000

500 meters

2000 feet

N →

THE PERSIAN EMPIRE DURING ESTHER'S TIME

While the story of Esther is enjoyed as one of the great dramas of the Bible, few readers understand that the world was at a historical crossroads during this time.

The Persian Empire extended from India to Ethiopia—even Egypt had fallen to the Persians. When the Persian Empire was at its height, major cultural developments were taking place throughout the world. Around the same time that Esther lived in Persia, Confucius lived in China, Buddha lived in India, and Socrates lived in Greece.

While Esther was alive, this gold relief panel (photo) was on display in Susa—the capital of the Persian Empire. Also during her lifetime, King Xerxes led the Persian army west in an effort to enter Europe and conquer Greece. The city states of Greece united to fight, hold off, and eventually defeat the Persians— handing them their first major military defeat. Had the Persians won that battle, their influence would have extended well into Europe. Instead, the Greek victory allowed the Greek culture and influence to rise and ultimately shape modern western civilization.

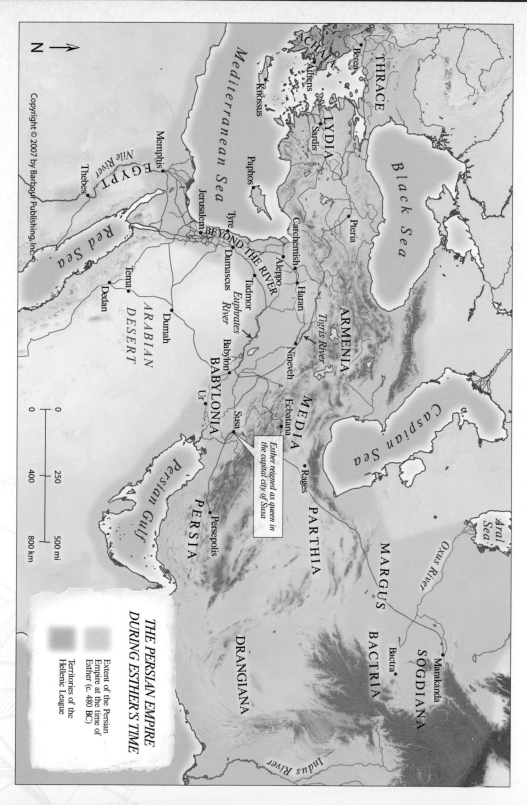

N →

Copyright © 2007 by Barbour Publishing, Inc.

Mediterranean Sea

THRACE

ACHAIA
Berea
Athens

LYDIA
Sardis

Knossos

Paphos

Black Sea

Pteria

Nile River
EGYPT
Memphis
Thebes

Jerusalem
Tyre

Carchemish

Haran

Tigris River

ARMENIA

Red Sea

BEYOND THE RIVER

Aleppo

Tadmor
Damascus
Euphrates River

Nineveh

MEDIA

Caspian Sea

Tema
Dedan

Dumah

ARABIAN DESERT

Babylon

BABYLONIA

Ur
Susa

Echatana

Esther reigned as queen in
the capital city of Susa

Rages

PARTHIA

Aral Sea

Oxus River

MARGUS

Bactra
BACTRIA

Marakanda
SOGDIANA

Persian Gulf

PERSIA

Persepolis

DRANGIANA

Indus River

0   0
400   250
800 km   500 mi

THE PERSIAN EMPIRE
DURING ESTHER'S TIME

Extent of the Persian
Empire at the time of
Esther (c. 480 BC)

Territories of the
Hellenic League

THE SETTING OF JOB

Job lived during a time when wealth was not measured in shekels or dollars but in herds and livestock. Job's thousands of sheep, oxen, and donkeys indicated that he was very, very rich.

Job's story is one of the most well-known in the Bible. His faith in God was tested when his children were killed and his wealth stripped from him. Job cursed the day he was born, yet he never disavowed his allegiance to God. In the end, God rewarded Job's faith by granting him a new family and doubling his original wealth.

Though the exact time of Job's story isn't known, the emphasis on livestock as a measurement of wealth seems to indicate that the story took place during or before the time of Abraham. And while the exact location of Job's story isn't indicated either, the presence of Sabean and Chaldean raiders suggest that Uz is located as indicated on the map.

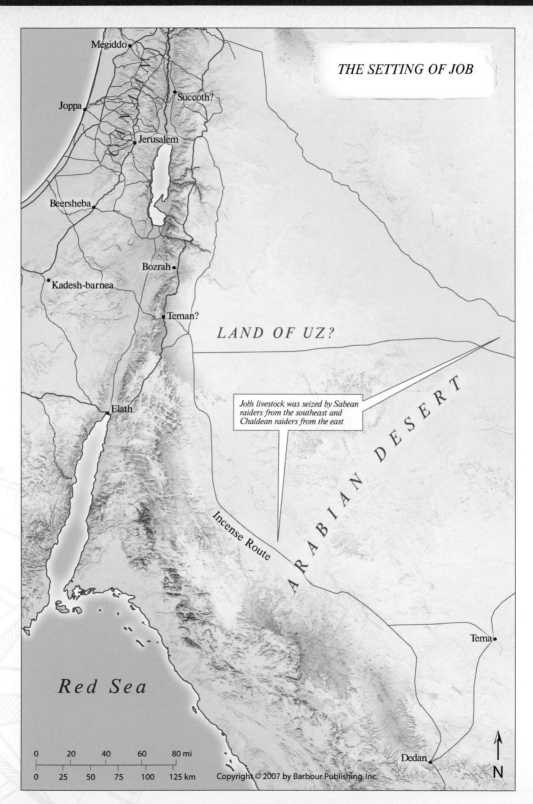

THE SETTING OF JOB

Megiddo

Joppa

Succoth?

Jerusalem

Beersheba

Bozrah

Kadesh-barnea

Teman?

LAND OF UZ?

Elath

Job's livestock was seized by Sabean raiders from the southeast and Chaldean raiders from the east

ARABIAN DESERT

Incense Route

Red Sea

Tema

0	20	40	60	80 mi
0	25	50	75	100	125 km

Copyright © 2007 by Barbour Publishing, Inc.

Dedan

N

THE PROPHETS

ASSYRIA ADVANCES ON JERUSALEM

Isaiah warned Israel of the impending danger from Assyria. The Judean oppression of the poor—depriving the needy of their rights—fueled God's discipline (Isaiah 10). Isaiah warned that nothing would save the Southern Kingdom from the coming judgment. When the people looked back and wondered why God allowed them to fall to the Assyrians, they would remember Isaiah's prophecy.

Were the Assyrians God's new people? No, they were merely the instrument God used to dole out His judgment (Isaiah 10:5). In fact, God pledged to discipline the Assyrians as well for their arrogance and pride. "When the Lord has finished all his work against Mount Zion and Jerusalem, he will say, 'I will punish the king of Assyria for the willfull pride of his heart and the haughty look in his eyes'" (Isaiah 10:12).

The map indicates the route the Assyrian army would take as envisioned by Isaiah. Michmash (see photo) stood at a natural crossroads that made it a strategic location on the north/south route through the land. For this reason, it was the location of several important battles (see page 54) and a tactical place for storing supplies (Isaiah 10:28).

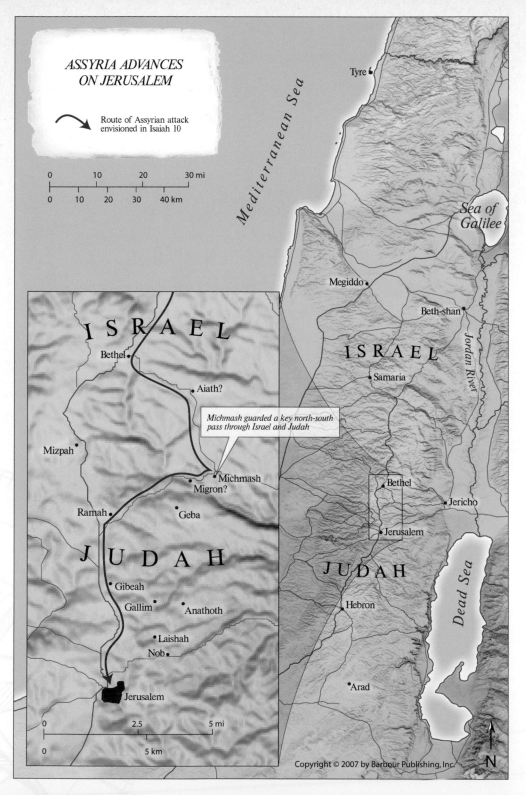

ASSYRIA ADVANCES ON JERUSALEM

Route of Assyrian attack envisioned in Isaiah 10

0   10   20   30 mi

0   10   20   30   40 km

Mediterranean Sea

Tyre

Sea of Galilee

Megiddo

Beth-shan

ISRAEL

Samaria

Jordan River

I S R A E L

Bethel

Aiath?

Michmash guarded a key north-south pass through Israel and Judah

Mizpah

Michmash

Migron?

Bethel

Jericho

Ramah

Geba

J U D A H

Jerusalem

Gibeah

Gallim

Anathoth

JUDAH

Laishah

Nob

Hebron

Dead Sea

Jerusalem

0   2.5   5 mi

0   5 km

Arad

N

PROPHECIES AGAINST MOAB

After the death of Ahab, Moab revolted against Israel's rule and gained independence. Even though Moab experienced immediate success in expanding its borders, Isaiah prophesied against the land of Moab and revealed that disaster would swiftly fall upon it (see Isaiah 15:1–16:4).

Moab contained diverse terrain—including both plush, green pastures and dry rocky areas (see photos). Moab is also distinguished in the Bible as the homeland of Ruth.

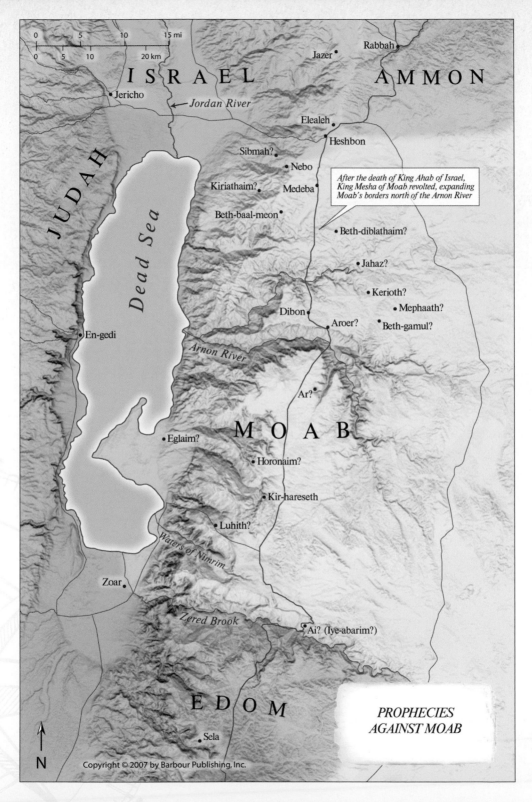

ISRAEL

AMMON

Jazer

Rabbah

Jericho

Jordan River

Elealeh

Heshbon

Sibmah?

Nebo

JUDAH

Kiriathaim?

Medeba

Dead Sea

After the death of King Ahab of Israel,
King Mesha of Moab revolted, expanding
Moab's borders north of the Arnon River

Beth-baal-meon

Beth-diblathaim?

Jahaz?

Kerioth?

Mephaath?

Dibon

Beth-gamul?

En-gedi

Aroer?

Arnon River

Ar?

M O A B

Eglaim?

Horonaim?

Kir-hareseth

Luhith?

Waters of Nimrim

Zoar

Zered Brook

Ai? (Iye-abarim?)

E D O M

PROPHECIES
AGAINST MOAB

N

Sela

Copyright © 2007 by Barbour Publishing, Inc.

GEDALIAH'S ASSASSINATION

Jeremiah eventually witnessed the fall of Jerusalem to Nebuchadnezzar's mighty Babylonian Empire. This empire was the dominant power in the Near East during this time. Without the luxuries of modern-day travel or communication, however, Nebuchadnezzar faced the challenges of ruling a vast empire from his own capital city. Because he needed a ruler who would stay faithful to him, the Babylonian king appointed Gedaliah to rule Judah.

Gedaliah tried to create order by assuring the Judeans who remained in the land, "Do not be afraid to serve the Babylonians. . . . Settle down in the land and serve the king of Babylon, and it will go well with you" (Jeremiah 40:9).

But Ishmael, a member of the Ammonite royal family, assassinated Gedaliah and other members of the court—throwing the dead bodies into a nearby cistern (see photo of a cistern of that day). Rather than kill every citizen, he also took captive a number of people who lived in Mizpah. Johanan, a man who had served Gedaliah faithfully, pursued Ishmael and recovered the prisoners. Ishmael, fearing for his life, fled to Ammon.

Through divine revelation, Jeremiah saw that this sequence of events could initiate the restoration of freedom for Judah (Jeremiah 42:10–12). He tried to convince the people to remain in the land and watch God restore their prosperity. The people, however,

feared retribution from the king of Babylon and many fled to Egypt. Rather than find the freedom and safety they were seeking, the people who fled to Egypt died of plagues and other disasters. (Read the full story in 2 Kings 25:25 and Jeremiah 40–42.)

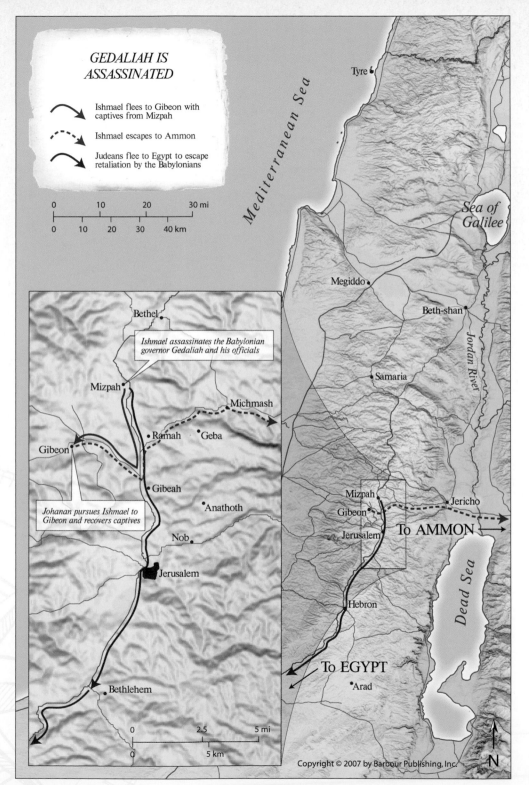

GEDALIAH IS ASSASSINATED

→ Ishmael flees to Gibeon with captives from Mizpah

⇢ Ishmael escapes to Ammon

↷ Judeans flee to Egypt to escape retaliation by the Babylonians

| 0 | 10 | 20 | 30 mi |
| 0 | 10 | 20 | 30 | 40 km |

Mediterranean Sea

Tyre

Sea of Galilee

Megiddo

Beth-shan

Jordan River

Samaria

Bethel

Ishmael assassinates the Babylonian governor Gedaliah and his officials

Mizpah

Michmash

Ramah • Geba

Gibeon

Gibeah

Johanan pursues Ishmael to Gibeon and recovers captives

Anathoth

Nob

Jerusalem

Mizpah

Gibeon

Jerusalem

Jericho

To AMMON

Dead Sea

Hebron

Bethlehem

To EGYPT

• Arad

N

121

TYRE'S INTERNATIONAL TRADE

Tyre—a city to Israel's north—was well-known throughout the world for its trade. Tyre's seaport became a distribution point for its wood, purple dye, precious metals, and other natural resources. In addition to moving their own commercial goods, the Phoenicians who lived there built a prosperous economy buying and selling goods from around the world. (See photo for their sunset view over the Mediterranean.) The map indicates the breadth of the trading completed by those who lived in this seaport city. Ezekiel 27–28 recounts the vastness of the trade, listing the cities and items traded within their economy. The Bible recounts that Tyre was "situated at the gateway to the sea" and was the "merchant of people on many coasts" (Ezekiel 27:3).

Tyre's economic prosperity, however, could not purchase God's favor. Because of the people's sin, arrogance, and hard hearts, God pronounced judgment on the city. Ezekiel the prophet warned: "Because you think you are wise, as wise as a god, I [God] am going to bring foreigners against you, the most ruthless of nations; they will draw their swords against your beauty and wisdom and pierce your shining splendor. They will bring you down to the pit, and you will die a violent death in the heart of the seas" (Ezekiel 28:6–8).

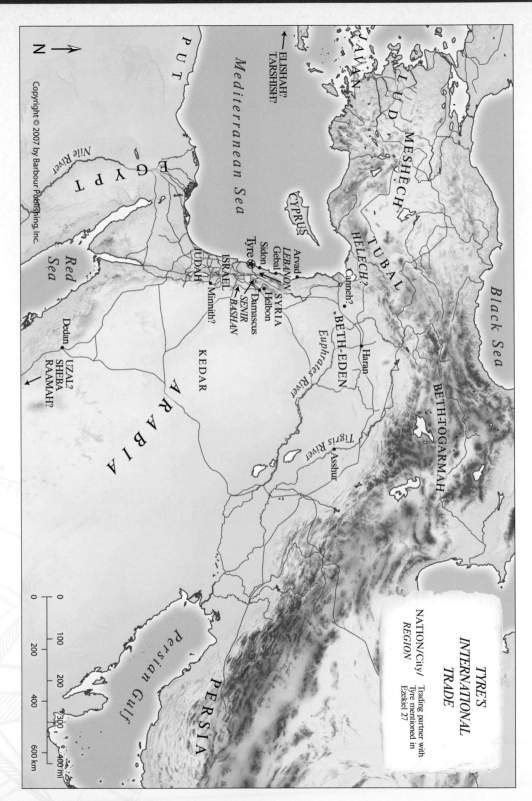

Copyright © 2007 by Barbour Publishing, Inc.

N →

**TYRE'S
INTERNATIONAL
TRADE**

NATION/City/
REGION

Trading partner with
Tyre mentioned in
Ezekiel 27

Mediterranean Sea

Nile River

Red Sea

PUT

EGYPT

CYPRUS

ELISHAH?
TARSHISH?

JAVAN

LUD

MESHECH

TUBAL

HELECH?

Black Sea

Arvad
LEBANON
Gebal
Sidon
Tyre
Canneh?

Helbon
Damascus
SYRIA
SENIR
BASHAN

JUDAH
ISRAEL
Minnith?

BETH-EDEN

Haran

Euphrates River

Asshur

Tigris River

BETH-TOGARMAH

Dedan

UZAL?
SHEBA
RAAMAH?

ARABIA

KEDAR

PERSIA

Persian Gulf

0   100   200   400   600 km
0   200   300   400 mi

EZEKIEL'S VISION OF ISRAEL'S NEW BOUNDARIES

Ezekiel 47:13–48:35 records part of the prophet's apocalyptic vision. Because the temple Ezekiel envisioned has not yet been built, this vision seems to point to a future time.

At the time of his vision, Ezekiel's audience lived in exile. His message of a future home that was free from any potential defeat and threat of exile would have found an eager audience.

Ezekiel's temple stands in contrast to the other temples in Israel's history. Here are some of the important differences:

- There is no separate courtyard for gentiles.

- There is no reference to the temple artifacts used in traditional temple worship (for example, the table of showbread, lampstands, veil, laver, etc.).

- There is a miraculous, life-giving river that flows from the temple.

Many Christians draw connections between these differences and New Testament theology. For example, the New Testament includes all people equally into worship. Also, the river flowing from the temple in Ezekiel's vision is reminiscent of the river of life flowing from the throne of God in Revelation 22.

EZEKIEL'S VISION OF ISRAEL'S NEW BOUNDARIES

The boundaries of the Promised Land as envisioned by Ezekiel

The boundaries of the Promised Land as described in Numbers 34

| 0 | 20 | 40 | 60 mi |
| 0 | 20 | 40 | 60 | 80 km |

Mediterranean Sea

Hethlon

Zedad

Lebo-hamath

D A N

A S H E R

Sidon

N A P H T A L I

Damascus

Tyre

M A N A S S E H

E P H R A I M

HAURAN

Sea of Galilee

R E U B E N

Jordan River

G I L E A D

J U D A H

[S A C R E D]

Dead Sea

B E N J A M I N

En-gedi

S I M E O N

En-eglaim?

I S S A C H A R

Z E B U L U N

Brook of Egypt?

G A D

Tamar?

Kadesh

N

JUDAH		
← Mediterra-nean Sea	LEVITES	Jordan River →
PRINCE'S LAND	PRIESTS TEMPLE→■ CITY	PRINCE'S LAND
	FARMS ⌐⌐ FARMS	
BENJAMIN		

Copyright © 2007 by Barbour Publishing, Inc.

125

THE GREEK EMPIRES

During Daniel's time of service under the Medes and the Persians, he saw a vision that greatly disturbed him (Daniel 8:27), perhaps because it spoke about the demise of the empire he served. In his vision, he saw the rise of the Greek Empire and its swift spread across the world (Daniel 8:5). That vision came true two hundred years after Daniel lived—when Alexander the Great conquered the world in twelve short years. (See photo of an ancient representation of Alexander the Great.)

Daniel's vision also foretold that the leader of Greece "at the height of his power. . .was broken off, and in its place four prominent horns grew up" (Daniel 8:8). As if following the script, Alexander the Great died at age thirty-two and his kingdom fell into a power struggle among his various generals. Eventually the borders came to resemble those shown on this map, with Cassander ruling in the east, Lysimachus ruling in the north by the Black Sea, Antigonus ruling in the center, Ptolemy ruling in the south, and Seleucus ruling in the east. Later Seleucus defeated Antigonus and claimed the area of Asia Minor for himself.

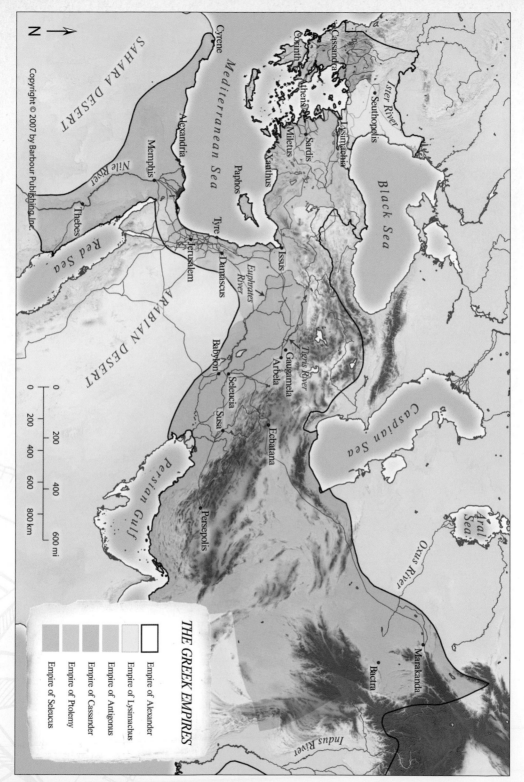

THE GREEK EMPIRES

Empire of Alexander
Empire of Lysimachus
Empire of Antigonus
Empire of Cassander
Empire of Ptolemy
Empire of Seleucus

N →

SAHARA DESERT

Mediterranean Sea

Nile River

Red Sea

ARABIAN DESERT

Persian Gulf

Black Sea

Caspian Sea

Aral Sea

Ister River

Euphrates River

Tigris River

Oxus River

Indus River

Cyrene
Corinth
Cassandra
Athens
Miletus
Sardis
Lysimachia
Seuthopolis
Paphos
Xanthus
Alexandria
Memphis
Thebes
Tyre
Jerusalem
Damascus
Issus
Babylon
Gaugamela
Arbela
Seleucia
Susa
Ecbatana
Persepolis
Marakanda
Bactra

0   200   400   600   800 km
0   200   400   600 mi

127

THE PTOLEMAIC AND THE SELEUCID EMPIRES (EARLY)

Daniel 11 unfolds another account of a prophetic vision seen by Daniel. Daniel 11:5 reads, "The king of the South will become strong, but one of his commanders will become even stronger than he and will rule his own kingdom with great power." This prophecy was fulfilled when Ptolemy's general, Seleucus, began to conquer the lands originally taken by Alexander and then divided by the other generals. Soon the Seleucid empire was established, which was greater than Ptolemy's territory in the south.

The photo on this page is of Acco/Ptolemais near sunset. Mt. Carmel is located in the background.

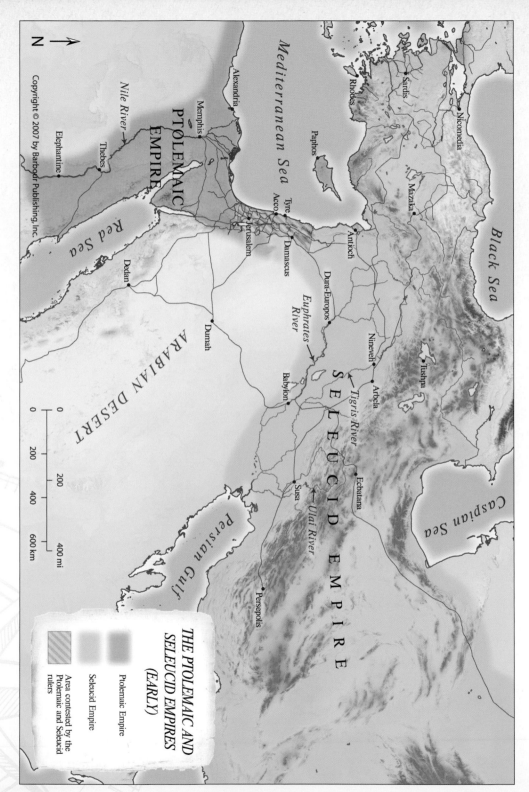

N →

Copyright © 2007 by Barbour Publishing, Inc.

Mediterranean Sea

Alexandria

Memphis

PTOLEMAIC
EMPIRE

Nile River →

Thebes

Elephantine

Red Sea

ARABIAN DESERT

Dedan

Dumah

Rhodes

Sardis

Nicomedia

Paphos

Mazaka

Tyre

Acco

Jerusalem

Damascus

Antioch

Dura-Europos

*Euphrates
River* →

Babylon

Nineveh

Arbela

Tigris River →

Tushpa

Ecbatana

Susa

Ulai River →

SELEUCID EMPIRE

Black Sea

Caspian Sea

Persian Gulf

Persepolis

0
0
200
200
400
400
600 km
400 mi

*THE PTOLEMAIC AND
SELEUCID EMPIRES
(EARLY)*

Ptolemaic Empire

Seleucid Empire

Area contested by the
Ptolemaic and Seleucid
rulers

THE NEAR EAST DURING THE TIME OF THE MACCABEES

Daniel 11:21–35 almost certainly predicts the rise of Antiochus Epiphanes. Further records of the events of this time are found in the extra-biblical books of the Maccabees.

Many Bible scholars also interpret Daniel 8:9–13 as a reference to Antiochus Epiphanes. History recounts that he ruled the land of Israel cruelly beginning in 167 BC. Because the Seleucid kingdom was beginning to wane (compare map on previous page with the map on next page), Antiochus tried to tighten his grip on his occupied territory by enforcing conformity and uniformity in religion and the Greek culture. Some of his escapades include:

- Sending twenty-two thousand soldiers to Jerusalem under the guise of a peace mission. However, they attacked the city on the Sabbath and slaughtered the people.

- He tried to Hellenize the Jewish people by ridding the land of temple worship.

- He burned copies of the Torah.

- He outlawed Jewish rites and customs such as circumcision.

- He erected an altar to Zeus on the temple mount, sacrificing a pig on it.

This final action is considered by many to be "the abomination that causes desolation" that is referenced in Daniel 8 and 11.

Within three years after this ultimate abomination, the Jewish people broke free from their oppressors and established an independent kingdom ruled by the Maccabeans. This kingdom lasted about one hundred years until Rome conquered the city in 63 BC. The photo above is of the traditional tombs of the Maccabees.

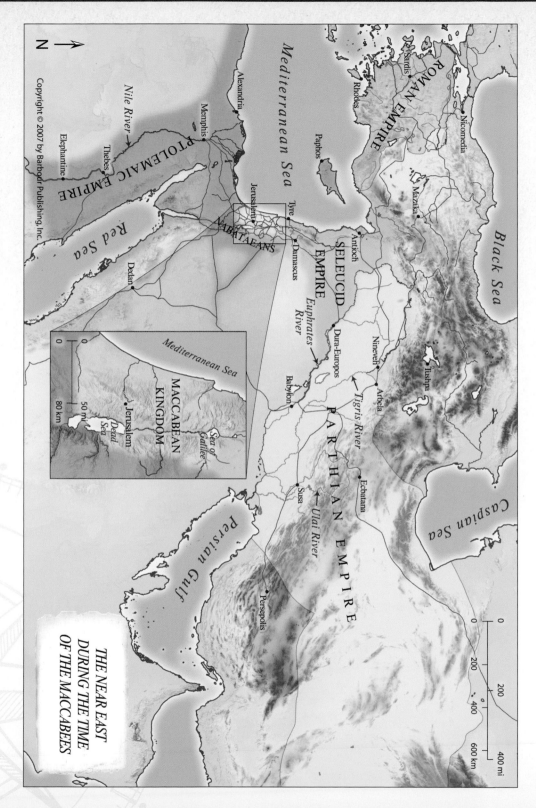

N →

Copyright © 2007 by Barbour Publishing, Inc.

Mediterranean Sea

Nile River

Alexandria

Memphis

Elephantine
Thebes

PTOLEMAIC EMPIRE

Red Sea

Dedan

Jerusalem
Tyre

NABATAEANS

Damascus

SELEUCID EMPIRE

Euphrates River

Paphos

Antioch

Dura-Europos

Babylon

ROMAN EMPIRE

Sardis
Rhodes

Nicomedia

Mazaka

Nineveh

Arbela

Tushpa

Black Sea

Tigris River

Ecbatana

Susa

Ulai River

PARTHIAN EMPIRE

Persepolis

Caspian Sea

Persian Gulf

Mediterranean Sea

MACCABEAN KINGDOM

Jerusalem

Dead Sea

Sea of Galilee

0   0
        50 mi
80 km

0   0   200   400   600 km
        200   400   600 mi

**THE NEAR EAST
DURING THE TIME
OF THE MACCABEES**

131

THE PROPHETS OF ISRAEL AND JUDAH

Many books in the Old Testament overview the reigns of the kings of the Northern and Southern Kingdoms. And while important, no recount of their history would be complete without remembering the prophets who served as God's mouthpieces during their reigns. Below are many of the major biblical prophets with references to the kings they served.

Key Prophets	The Kings They Primarily Served
Ahijah	Solomon and Jeroboam of the northern kingdom of Israel
Jehu	Baasha, Elah, and Zimri of Israel
Elijah	Ahab and Ahaziah of Israel
Elisha	Ahaziah, Jehu, and Jehoash of Israel
Jonah	Jeroboam II of Israel
Hosea	Jeroboam II (of Israel); Uzziah, Jotham, Ahaz, and Hezekiah (all of Judah)
Amos	Jeroboam II of Israel
Isaiah	Ahaz and Hezekiah of Judah
Micah	Jotham, Ahaz, and Hezekiah of Judah
Jeremiah	Josiah, Jehoahaz, Jehoiakim, Jehoiachin, and Zedekiah
Zephaniah	Josiah of Judah
Nahum	Josiah of Judah
Zechariah and Haggai	Served during reconstruction of temple after captivity
Malachi	Served after the people returned from exile
Prophets with unknown locations	
Joel	Uncertain
Obadiah	Uncertain
Habakkuk	Josiah of Judah
Prophets whose primary ministry occurred outside the promised land	
Ezekiel and Daniel	Primarily served while people were in exile

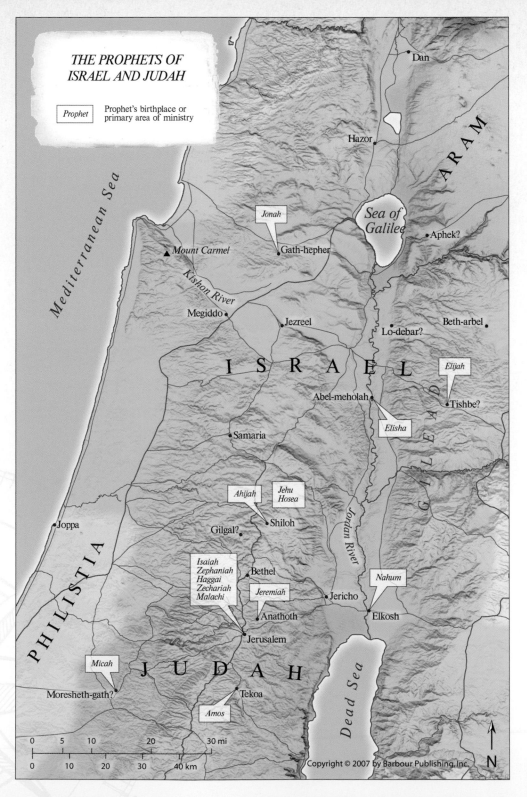

THE PROPHETS OF
ISRAEL AND JUDAH

Prophet — Prophet's birthplace or primary area of ministry

Dan

ARAM

Hazor

Mediterranean Sea

Jonah

Sea of Galilee

Aphek?

Mount Carmel

Gath-hepher

Kishon River

Megiddo

Jezreel

Lo-debar?

Beth-arbel

ISRAEL

Elijah

Abel-meholah

Tishbe?

Elisha

GILEAD

Samaria

Ahijah

Jehu
Hosea

Gilgal?

Shiloh

Jordan River

Joppa

Isaiah
Zephaniah
Haggai
Zechariah
Malachi

Bethel

Nahum

Jeremiah

Jericho

PHILISTIA

Anathoth

Elkosh

Jerusalem

Micah

J U D A H

Dead Sea

Moresheth-gath?

Tekoa

Amos

0   5   10   20   30 mi

0   10   20   30   40 km

Copyright © 2007 by Barbour Publishing, Inc.

N

THE NEW TESTAMENT

THE HOLY LAND IN THE TIME OF JESUS

Herod the Great ruled the land of Israel during the time of Jesus' birth. Called "King Herod," he had been appointed to his office by the Senate in Rome.

A paranoid ruler, Herod maintained power at times by violence. He executed one of his wives and murdered his sister's husband. When he felt threatened by his nephew, he marshaled his troops against him. He also married his own niece to secure his power. He also went as far as killing three of his own sons. With this background, it is not surprising that he issued a death sentence to a few baby boys living in the small town of Bethlehem—the town which was the purported home of a newly-born king (Luke 2).

While known for his use of strong force, Herod was also recognized as a master architect. Herod rebuilt the temple in Jerusalem, expanded the city walls, built a fortress at Masada, expanded the country's water supplies, and built a number of beautiful buildings throughout Israel that still stand (at least in part) today.

The photograph on this page shows walls and a tower known as the Citadel of David. This tower and portion of the wall were built by Herod the Great and would have been one of the views Jesus saw in Jerusalem.

At Herod's death, the country was divided between his three sons and each ruled over his own region (as indicated on the map).

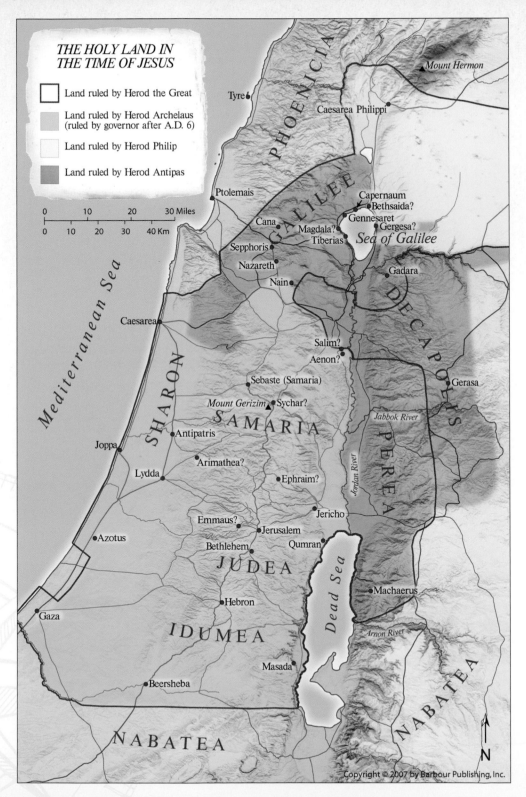

THE HOLY LAND IN
THE TIME OF JESUS

Land ruled by Herod the Great

Land ruled by Herod Archelaus
(ruled by governor after A.D. 6)

Land ruled by Herod Philip

Land ruled by Herod Antipas

0   10   20   30 Miles

0   10   20   30   40 Km

PHOENICIA

Mount Hermon

Tyre

Caesarea Philippi

Ptolemais

Capernaum
Bethsaida?
Gennesaret
Cana   Gergesa?
Magdala?   Sea of Galilee
Sepphoris   Tiberias
Nazareth
GALILEE
Nain   Gadara

Mediterranean Sea

Caesarea

DECAPOLIS

Salim?
Aenon?

Sebaste (Samaria)   Gerasa

Mount Gerizim Sychar?

Jabbok River

SHARON

SAMARIA   PEREA

Joppa   Antipatris

Arimathea?

Lydda   Ephraim?   Jordan River

Emmaus?   Jericho

Azotus   Jerusalem
Bethlehem   Qumran

JUDEA   Dead Sea

Hebron

Machaerus

Gaza   IDUMEA   Arnon River

Masada

NABATEA

Beersheba

NABATEA

N

Copyright © 2007 by Barbour Publishing, Inc.

137

JESUS' MINISTRY IN GALILEE AND BEYOND

Since the days that Jesus lived on earth, people of all faiths have claimed to control the traditional sites of key Bible events or locations that have been considered holy. In many cases, a church or other memorial was built over the location to preserve the ancient memory of Jesus or His disciples. For example, the photos on this page show a modern church that was built over the home thought to be Peter's house. The photos reveal the care taken in building the church while leaving the remains of the house and later church buildings undisturbed.

Below are some of the events of Jesus' ministry that are listed on the map. Many of these locations are also marked with memorials and churches:
- Jesus heals the daughter of a Syrian Phoenician woman—Matthew 15; Mark 7
- The Transfiguration—Matthew 17; Mark 9; Luke 9
- Peter's confession—Matthew 16; Mark 8; Luke 9
- Jesus turns water into wine—John 2
- Feeding of the multitudes—Matthew 15; Mark 8; Luke 9; John 6
- Jesus casts demons into pigs—Matthew 8; Mark 5; Luke 8
- Jesus walks on water—Matthew 14; Mark 6; John 6
- Jesus raises a widow's son from the dead—Luke 7
- Jesus heals a man in the Decapolis—Mark 7
- Jesus heals ten lepers—Luke 17

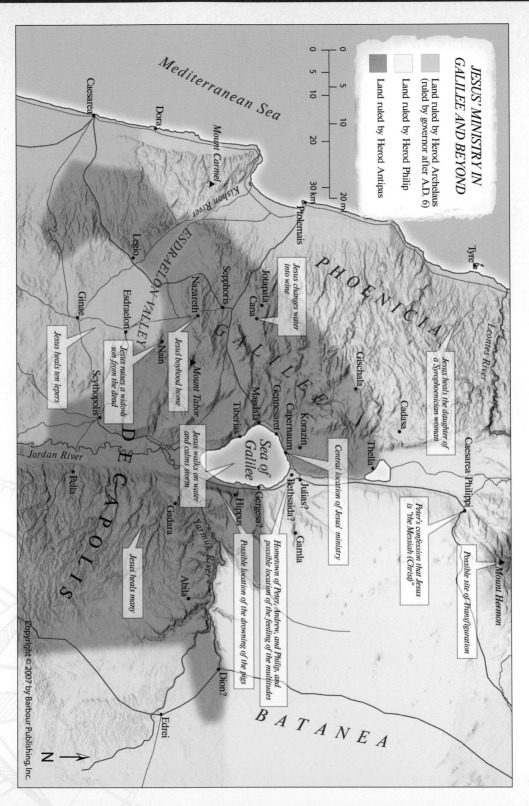

JESUS' MINISTRY IN GALILEE AND BEYOND

Land ruled by Herod Archelaus (ruled by governor after A.D. 6)
Land ruled by Herod Philip
Land ruled by Herod Antipas

Mediterranean Sea

Caesarea
Dora
Mount Carmel
Kishon River
ESDRAELON VALLEY
Legio
Ginae
Estraelon
Nazareth
Sepphoris
Jotapata
Cana
Ptolemais
Tyre

PHOENICIA
Leontes River
Gischala
Cadasa
Thella

GALILEE
Nain
Mount Tabor
Scythopolis
Tiberias
Magdala
Gennesaret
Capernaum
Korazin
Sea of Galilee
Gergesa?
Bethsaida?
Julias?
Gamla
Hippus
Gadara
Abila
Yarmuk River

DECAPOLIS
Jordan River
Pella
Dion?
Edrei

BATANEA

Caesarea Philippi
Mount Hermon

Jesus changes water into wine

Jesus heals the daughter of a Syrophoenician woman

Central location of Jesus' ministry

Peter's confession that Jesus is "the Messiah (Christ)"

Possible site of Transfiguration

Jesus heals ten lepers

Jesus raises a widow's son from the dead

Jesus' boyhood home

Jesus walks on water and calms storm

Possible location of the drowning of the pigs

Hometown of Peter, Andrew, and Philip, and possible location of the feeding of the multitudes

Jesus heals many

0 5 10 20 30 km
0 5 10 20 m

N →

Copyright © 2007 by Barbour Publishing, Inc.

139

THE LAST SUPPER

On the night before His death, Jesus and His disciples met in an upper room to eat the Passover meal together. This final meal has become known as the "Last Supper." The first photo below shows the room traditionally believed to be the location where Jesus and His disciples gathered for this meal.

Upon completing dinner, Jesus and His disciples went to the Garden of Gethsemane where Jesus spent considerable time in prayer. Though the olive trees currently in this garden are very old—perhaps even fifteen hundred years old—they are not the same trees from Jesus' time. The Romans destroyed all of the trees around Jerusalem in AD 70.

The garden stands at the foot of the Mount of Olives, which is mentioned during the events of the holy week as well as in the story of King David. King David traveled to this mountain when Absalom led a revolt against him (2 Samuel 15:30).

Today the Mount of Olives is the site of many churches commemorating events in Jesus' life.

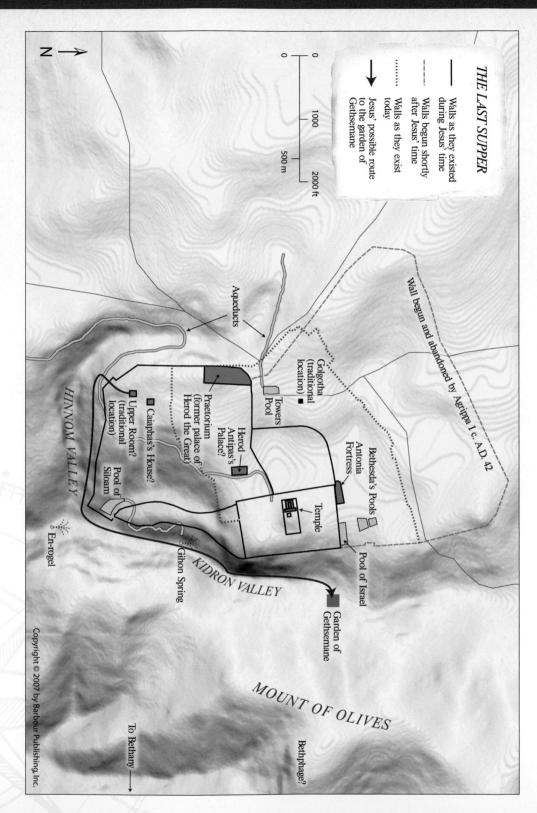

THE LAST SUPPER

N →

	Walls as they existed during Jesus' time
	Walls begun shortly after Jesus' time
	Walls as they exist today
↓	Jesus' possible route to the garden of Gethsemane

0 1000 2000 ft
0 500 m

Aqueducts

Wall begun and abandoned by Agrippa I c. A.D. 42

Golgotha (traditional location)

Towers Pool

Praetorium (former palace of Herod the Great)

Herod Antipas's Palace?

Upper Room? (traditional location)

Caiaphas's House?

HINNOM VALLEY

Pool of Siloam

En-rogel

Gihon Spring

KIDRON VALLEY

Antonia Fortress

Bethesda's Pools

Temple

Pool of Israel

Garden of Gethsemane

MOUNT OF OLIVES

To Bethany

Bethphage?

JESUS' ARREST, TRIAL, AND CRUCIFIXION

Though the Jewish religious leaders wanted to put Jesus to death, they may not have had the civil authority to do so. Having found Jesus guilty in their own Jewish court, they also pursued a civil trial which would yield the death sentence they sought.

Although they recognized the Jewish leaders' motives, Herod Antipas and Pilate also knew that Jesus was a popular teacher among the people. This caused them to treat Jesus' trial with political gamesmanship—neither leader wanting to take the responsibility for condemning the popular teacher. And while they wanted to appease the Jewish leaders, they did not want to appear to be too heavily influenced by these men. Below is a list of events that occurred during Jesus' last days.

Event	Biblical Reference
The Last Supper	Matthew 26:20–30; Mark 14:17–26; Luke 22:14–38; John 13–14
Jesus arrested	Matthew 26:47–56; Mark 14:43–52; Luke 22:47–53; John 18:1–12
Jesus found guilty by Jewish leaders	Matthew 27:1–2; Mark 15:1; Luke 22:66–71
Jesus before Pilate for first trial	Matthew 27:11–14; Mark 15:2–5; Luke 23:1–5; John 18:28–37
Pilate defers Jesus' case to Herod Antipas	Luke 23:6–12
Herod returns Jesus to Pilate	Luke 23:11
Pilate sentences Jesus to death	Matthew 27:26; Mark 15:15; Luke 23:23–24; John 19:16
Jesus crucified	Matthew 27:32–34; Mark 15:21–25; Luke 23:26–34; John 19:16–24
Jesus buried in tomb of Joseph of Arimathea	Matthew 27:57–61; Mark 15:42–47; Luke 23:50–56; John 19:38–42
Jesus' resurrection	Matthew 28:1–3, Mark 16:1–8, Luke 24:1–12, John 20:1–9

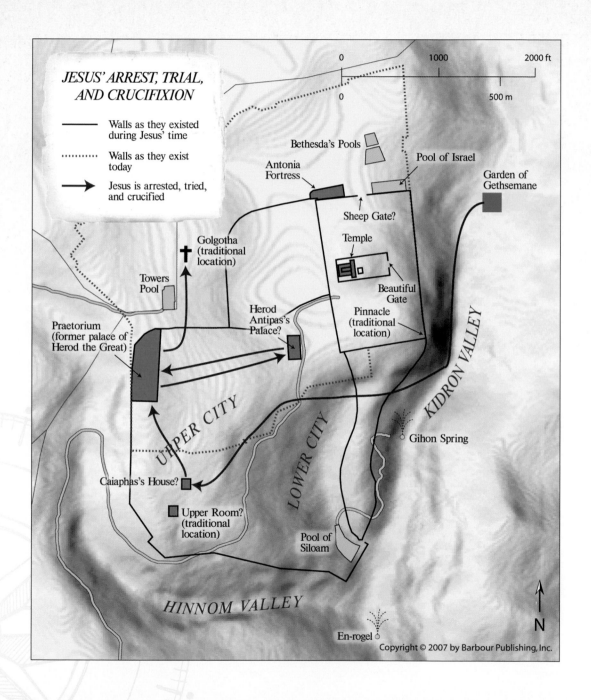

JESUS' ARREST, TRIAL, AND CRUFIFIXION

——— Walls as they existed during Jesus' time

·········· Walls as they exist today

→ Jesus is arrested, tried, and crucified

0   1000   2000 ft

0   500 m

Bethesda's Pools

Antonia Fortress

Pool of Israel

Garden of Gethsemane

Sheep Gate?

Golgotha (traditional location)

Temple

Towers Pool

Beautiful Gate

Praetorium (former palace of Herod the Great)

Herod Antipas's Palace?

Pinnacle (traditional location)

KIDRON VALLEY

UPPER CITY

Gihon Spring

Caiaphas's House?

LOWER CITY

Upper Room? (traditional location)

Pool of Siloam

HINNOM VALLEY

En-rogel

N

Copyright © 2007 by Barbour Publishing, Inc.

THE JOURNEY TO EMMAUS

Luke 24:13–32 records the story of Jesus' post-resurrection appearance to two disciples as they walked to Emmaus. The story takes place just after several of Jesus' followers had visited His tomb and found it empty. Not only was the tomb empty, but some of the women said angels explained the empty tomb by reminding them that Jesus had said He would rise again on the third day. One of the women even claimed to have encountered Jesus personally.

It's clear by the demeanor of these two followers that either they were unsure about the validity of these reports or unsure about their meaning. Either way, they were disappointed that their original expectations for Jesus had not been met.

Along the way, Jesus joined them. His true identity was hidden from them either by physical changes to His body or by divine intervention. As they walked, Jesus explained to them the important purposes behind the crucifixion and resurrection. Just when Jesus opened their eyes and allowed them to recognize the identity of their traveling companion, He disappeared from their sight. Fueled by the emotion of their encounter, they risked travel by night to tell the disciples in Jerusalem what they had seen and learned.

Below is a list of many of the post-resurrection appearances of Jesus as they are recorded in the New Testament.

Appearance	Biblical Reference
Jesus appears to Mary at the tomb.	Matthew 28:9–10; Mark 16:9; John 20:10–17
Jesus appears (twice) to the disciples in a locked room.	Luke 24:36–48; John 20:19–29
Jesus appears to two followers on the road to Emmaus.	Mark 16:12–13; Luke 24:13–32
Jesus appears to seven of His disciples— including Peter—beside the Sea of Galilee.	John 21:1–23
Jesus appears to the eleven disciples and gives them the "Great Commission."	Matthew 28:16–20; Mark 16:18
Jesus appears to Peter.	Luke 24:34; 1 Corinthians 15:5
Jesus appears to 500 people at once.	1 Corinthians 15:6
Jesus appears to James.	1 Corinthians 15:7
Jesus ascends to heaven in the presence of many.	Mark 16:19–20; Luke 24:50–51; Acts 1:4–9
Jesus appears to Paul.	Acts 9:1–9; 1 Corinthians 15:8

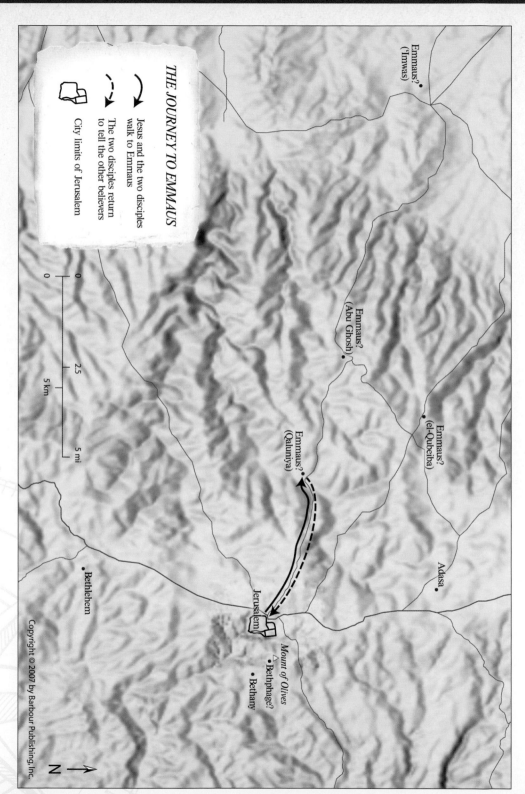

THE JOURNEY TO EMMAUS

Jesus and the two disciples walk to Emmaus

The two disciples return to tell the other believers

City limits of Jerusalem

Emmaus?
('Imwas)

Emmaus?
(Abu Ghosh)

Emmaus?
(el-Qubeiba)

Emmaus?
(Qaluniya)

Adasa

Bethlehem

Jerusalem

Mount of Olives
Bethphage?
Bethany

0   2.5   5 Km

0   5 mi

Copyright © 2007 by Barbour Publishing, Inc.

N

THE NATIONS AT PENTECOST

Pentecost, or the time of the "Harvest Offering," was one of the seven great feasts celebrated by the Jewish people (see Leviticus 23:15–22). With an international crowd on hand for the festival, God established the church by supernaturally empowering His disciples with the Holy Spirit. Acts 2 describes this incredible event and delineates the many nations represented in the crowd—each one hearing the gospel preached in their own native language (Acts 2:6–11). The map, showing the nations listed in Acts in red type, indicates the variety of languages represented by the thousands that attended this gathering.

This event marks a turning point in the New Testament: The first half of the New Testament records the life of Jesus, His death, and His resurrection. The outpouring of the Holy Spirit at Pentecost shifts the focus from the earthly life of Christ to the establishment of His church. Below is a timeline of major events that occurred in the New Testament:

4 BC or 5 BC	The birth of Jesus
AD 26–30	The public ministry of Jesus
AD 26	The ministry of John the Baptist begins
AD 30	The death and resurrection of Jesus
AD 33	The conversion of Saul of Tarsus
AD 47–48	Paul's first missionary journey (see page 154)
AD 50–52	Paul's second missionary journey (see page 156)
AD 53–57	Paul's final missionary journey (see page 158)

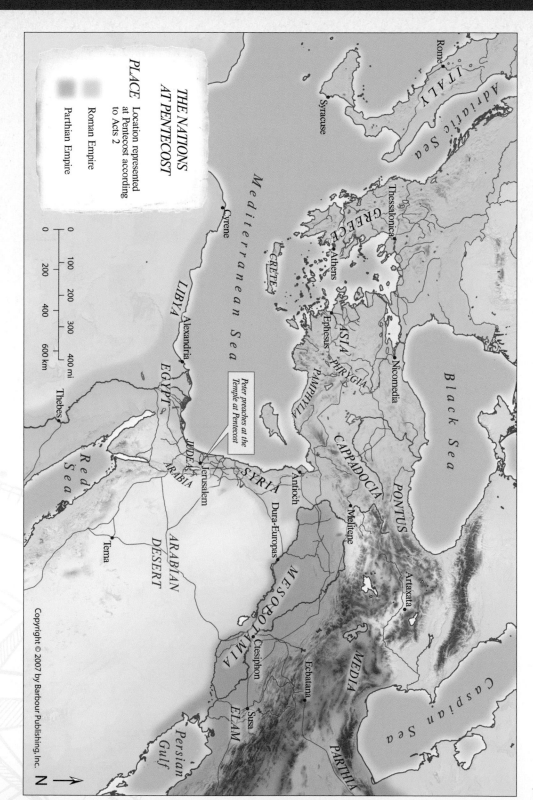

THE NATIONS
AT PENTECOST

PLACE Location represented
at Pentecost according
to Acts 2

Roman Empire

Parthian Empire

0
100
200 200
400 300
600 km 400 mi

0

Thebes

Copyright © 2007 by Barbour Publishing, Inc.

Rome
ITALY
Adriatic Sea
Syracuse
Mediterranean Sea
Thessalonica
GREECE
CRETE
Athens
Ephesus
ASIA
PHRYGIA
Nicomedia
PAMPHYLIA
Black Sea
Cyrene
LIBYA
Alexandria
EGYPT
CAPPADOCIA
PONTUS
Caspian Sea
Peter preaches at the
Temple at Pentecost
Red Sea
JUDEA
ARABIA
Jerusalem
SYRIA
Antioch
Dura-Europas
Melitene
Artaxata
Tema
ARABIAN
DESERT
MESOPOTAMIA
MEDIA
Ctesiphon
Ecbatana
Susa
ELAM
Persian
Gulf
PARTHIA

N →

PHILIP'S MINISTRY

Acts 8 records many events from the ministry of Philip, known through church history as "Philip the Evangelist." Driven from Jerusalem by the persecution against Christians, Philip preached the gospel in Samaria before returning to Jerusalem—the home base of the church. Once back in the city, God instructed Philip to travel to Gaza. Along the way, Philip met an official from the court of the Ethiopian queen. This man was reading from the Hebrew scriptures and trying to determine their meaning.

Philip interpreted the scriptures for him and told him about Jesus. Acts 8:38 records that the man put his faith in Christ, was baptized, and returned to Ethiopia. The Acts account then recounts how Philip was miraculously transported to the town of Azotus, where he continued preaching until he reached Caesarea.

The town of Caesarea was the Roman administrative center of the region and had been an important center for Herod the Great's building projects. A port city that would see many travelers, this town became an important showpiece for Herod and his projects. One of his most lasting structures is called the Hippodrome (see photo). This structure provided a powerful impression for travelers as they entered the city. With a seating capacity of thousands, this stadium was 250 yards long and 90 yards across. According to the Jewish historian Josephus, Herod Agrippa died while near this venue. Acts records the event this way: "Herod, wearing his royal robes, sat on his throne and delivered a public address to the people. They shouted, 'This is the voice of a god, not of a man.' Immediately, because Herod did not give praise to God, an angel of the Lord struck him down, and he was eaten by worms and died" (Acts 12:21–23).

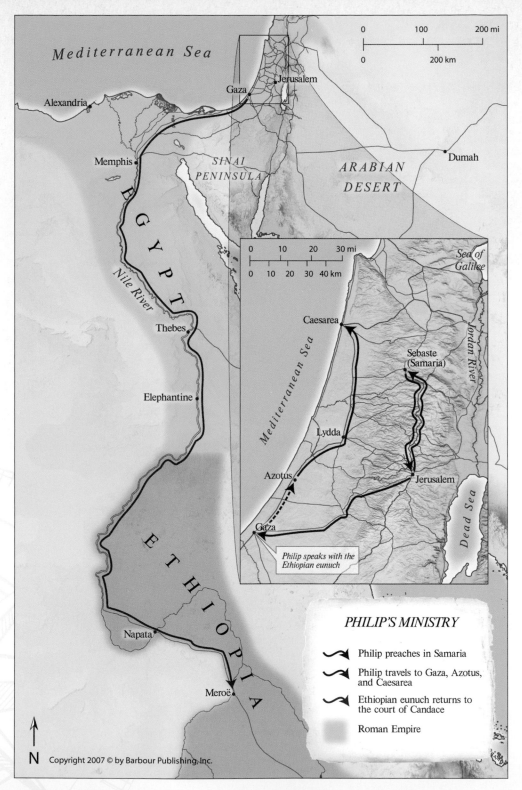

Mediterranean Sea

Alexandria

Gaza

Jerusalem

Dumah

Memphis

SINAI
PENINSULA

ARABIAN
DESERT

E
G
Y
P
T

Nile River

Thebes

Elephantine

E
T
H
I
O
P
I
A

Napata

Meroë

0   100   200 mi

0   200 km

Sea of
Galilee

0   10   20   30 mi

0   10   20   30   40 km

Caesarea

Sebaste
(Samaria)

Mediterranean Sea

Jordan River

Lydda

Azotus

Jerusalem

Gaza

Dead Sea

*Philip speaks with the
Ethiopian eunuch*

PHILIP'S MINISTRY

Philip preaches in Samaria

Philip travels to Gaza, Azotus,
and Caesarea

Ethiopian eunuch returns to
the court of Candace

Roman Empire

N

Copyright 2007 © by Barbour Publishing, Inc.

SAUL'S CONVERSION AND EARLY TRAVELS

It's difficult to imagine the story of the early church without Paul (originally known as Saul). This giant of Christian faith and history seems to be ever-present in the second half of the New Testament. The verses in Acts 9 and beyond read so matter-of-factly that it appears that Paul's public ministry began at the moment he converted to Christianity. The reality, however, is that Paul spent several years in preparation before becoming a traveling evangelist and prominent New Testament figure. Below is a list of events that occurred during Paul's early years as a Christian.

- The Jewish leaders give Paul permission to arrest Christians. Jesus appears to Paul during his journey to Damascus, leaving him blinded (Acts 9:1–9).
- Ananias prays for Paul and God restores his sight (Acts 9:17–18).
- Paul spends time in Arabia growing in his newfound faith (Galatians 1:17). While we don't know how long he was in Arabia, we do know that it was three years before Paul returned to Jerusalem (Galatians 1:18).
- With the help of Barnabas, Paul joins the church in Jerusalem (Acts 9:27).
- His life threatened, Paul escapes to Caesarea where he boards a ship to his home city of Tarsus (Acts 9:30).
- Paul lives in Tarsus for five or six years until Barnabas recruits him to travel to Antioch (Acts 11:25–26).

The city of Tarsus was an important Roman city with a rich heritage. The photo on this page shows the Cleopatra Gate which stands at the west end of Tarsus; this is where Anthony and Cleopatra marched into the city in 41 BC. The restoration process has kept the original structure intact but has covered much of the original stone facing.

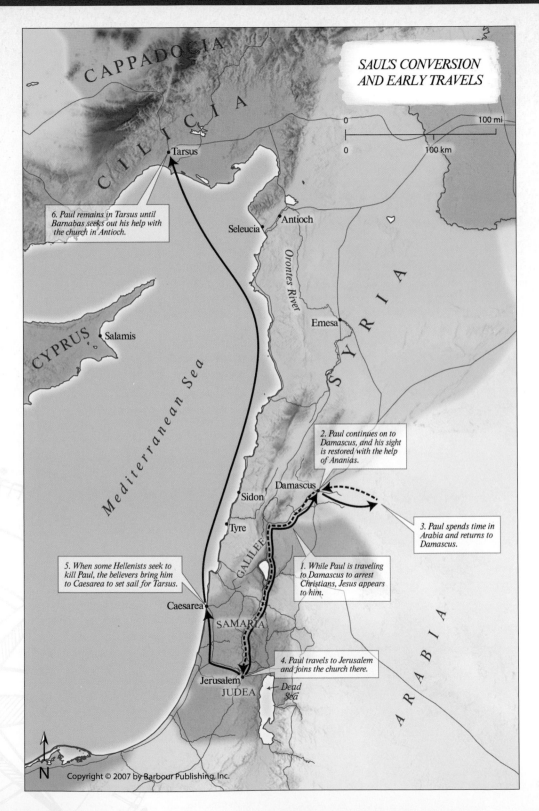

SAULS CONVERSION
AND EARLY TRAVELS

CAPPADOCIA

CILICIA

Tarsus

6. Paul remains in Tarsus until
Barnabas seeks out his help with
the church in Antioch.

Seleucia • Antioch

S Y R I A

Orontes River

Emesa

Mediterranean Sea

CYPRUS • Salamis

2. Paul continues on to
Damascus, and his sight
is restored with the help
of Ananias.

Damascus

Sidon

3. Paul spends time in
Arabia and returns to
Damascus.

Tyre

5. When some Hellenists seek to
kill Paul, the believers bring him
to Caesarea to set sail for Tarsus.

GALILEE

1. While Paul is traveling
to Damascus to arrest
Christians, Jesus appears
to him.

Caesarea

SAMARIA

A R A B I A

4. Paul travels to Jerusalem
and joins the church there.

Jerusalem
JUDEA

Dead
Sea

0   100 mi
0   100 km

N

Copyright © 2007 by Barbour Publishing, Inc.

PETER'S EARLY MINISTRY AND THE KINGDOM OF AGRIPPA I

Though a central figure in the early church in Jerusalem (Acts 1–12), Peter's ministry took him beyond the limits of the church's headquarters. Acts 9–10 records his visits to other cities and the boldness with which he shared the gospel message. These chapters capture three significant events in the ministry of Peter and of the early church:

- Peter heals a paralyzed man named Aeneas (Acts 9:33).
- Peter raises Dorcas from the dead in Joppa (Acts 9:40).
- Peter shares the gospel with Cornelius in Caesarea (Acts 10). Through this event with Cornelius, God brought Peter and the rest of the disciples to the realization that Gentiles were also to be welcomed as members of God's family.

Caesarea was an important city to Herod the Great (see page 148). As the access point to his kingdom for those coming from Rome, Herod made sure this city would impress visitors. As part of his building plan, Herod developed a forty-acre harbor, which accommo-

dated as many as three hundred ships. These building projects made Caesarea a well-traveled city and an important center for world trade and communication.

Many years after Cornelius's conversion, the apostle Paul was a prisoner in Caesarea (Acts 26). Approximately 125 years later, this city became the home of Origen, a Christian philosopher who lived between AD 185 and 254.

Through the teachings of Peter, Paul, and later Origen, Caesarea became both a symbolic and strategic location for the spread of the Christian faith.

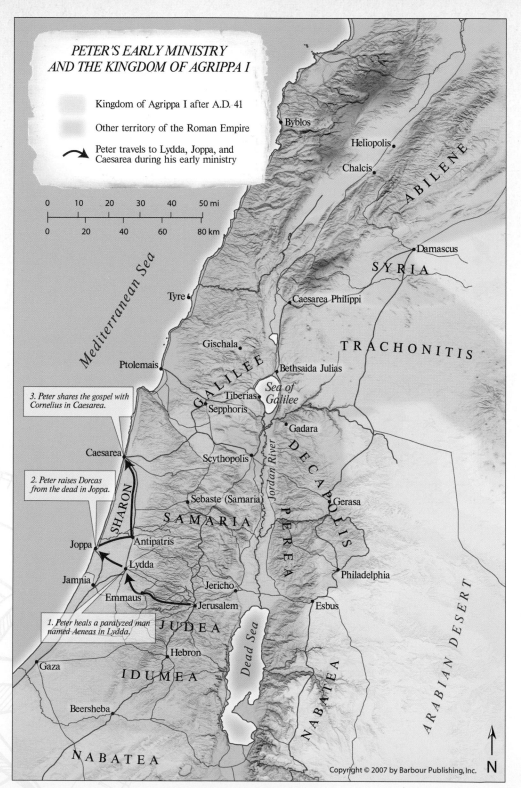

PETER'S EARLY MINISTRY
AND THE KINGDOM OF AGRIPPA I

Kingdom of Agrippa I after A.D. 41

Other territory of the Roman Empire

Peter travels to Lydda, Joppa, and
Caesarea during his early ministry

0   10   20   30   40   50 mi

0   20   40   60   80 km

Byblos

Heliopolis

Chalcis

ABILENE

Damascus

SYRIA

Mediterranean Sea

Tyre

Caesarea Philippi

Ptolemais

Gischala

GALILEE

TRACHONITIS

Bethsaida Julias

Sea of Galilee

3. Peter shares the gospel with
Cornelius in Caesarea.

Tiberias

Sepphoris

Gadara

Caesarea

Scythopolis

DECAPOLIS

Jordan River

2. Peter raises Dorcas
from the dead in Joppa.

SHARON

Sebaste (Samaria)

Gerasa

SAMARIA

PEREA

Joppa

Antipatris

Jamnia

Lydda

Emmaus

Jericho

Philadelphia

Jerusalem

Esbus

1. Peter heals a paralyzed man
named Aeneas in Lydda.

JUDEA

Dead Sea

Hebron

Gaza

IDUMEA

ARABIAN DESERT

NABATEA

Beersheba

NABATEA

N

Copyright © 2007 by Barbour Publishing, Inc.

PAUL'S FIRST MISSIONARY JOURNEY

When the church in Antioch decided to send a missionary team to preach Christ throughout other parts of the world, Barnabas went to Tarsus to recruit Paul for the work (Acts 11:25–26). Paul joined Barnabas in Antioch, and the two men (along with John Mark) traveled by ship on what has become known as Paul's first missionary journey. This trip most likely occurred in AD 47–48 and is chronicled in Acts 13–14.

The outbound portion of the trip focused on preaching Christ to the people within each of these cities and introducing them to Christianity. The inbound portion of the trip retraced the missionaries' steps in order to visit and encourage those who had become Christians during the first portion of their journey.

Some of the significant events that occurred during the first missionary journey include:

- Sergius Paulus, the governor of Cyprus, becomes a Christian (Acts 13:7).
- John Mark leaves Paul and Barnabas at Perga (Acts 13:13).
- Paul and Barnabas preach the gospel to the Gentiles in Pisidian Antioch (Acts 13:14).
- Paul is stoned in Lystra (Acts 14:19).

The photograph of the catacombs captures the influence of Christianity on the island of Cyprus. Though originally built as tombs, these underground rooms and tunnels were later converted to a Christian church.

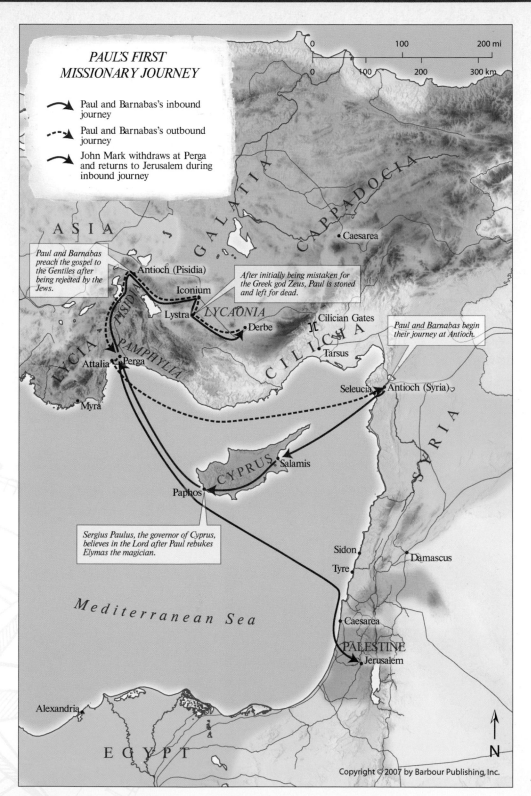

PAUL'S FIRST
MISSIONARY JOURNEY

Paul and Barnabas's inbound journey

Paul and Barnabas's outbound journey

John Mark withdraws at Perga and returns to Jerusalem during inbound journey

Paul and Barnabas preach the gospel to the Gentiles after being rejected by the Jews.

After initially being mistaken for the Greek god Zeus, Paul is stoned and left for dead.

Paul and Barnabas begin their journey at Antioch.

Sergius Paulus, the governor of Cyprus, believes in the Lord after Paul rebukes Elymas the magician.

ASIA

GALATIA

CAPPADOCIA

Caesarea

Antioch (Pisidia)

Iconium

Lystra

LYCAONIA

Derbe

Cilician Gates

Tarsus

PISIDIA

LYCIA

PAMPHYLIA

Attalia

Perga

Myra

CILICIA

Seleucia

Antioch (Syria)

SYRIA

CYPRUS

Salamis

Paphos

Sidon

Damascus

Tyre

Mediterranean Sea

Caesarea

PALESTINE

Jerusalem

Alexandria

EGYPT

N

0   100   200 mi
0   100   200   300 km

Copyright © 2007 by Barbour Publishing, Inc.

PAUL'S SECOND MISSIONARY JOURNEY

Paul's second missionary journey allowed him to revisit several churches he had established while on his way to Greece. This journey took place between AD 50 and 52 and is recorded in Acts 15–18.

While in Antioch preparing for their journey, Paul and Barnabas had a strong disagreement about the role of John Mark. Even though the young man had previously deserted them (Acts 13:13), Barnabas wanted to include him on this new trip—an idea Paul strongly opposed. The disagreement became so severe that Paul and Barnabas parted ways. Barnabas took John Mark and traveled to Cyprus, while Paul teamed up with Silas and continued his own journey west (Acts 15:39–41).

Early on, Paul spent time in Lystra. There he met Timothy who joined the missionary team for the rest of the journey (Acts 16:1–3). Their longest stay was in Corinth (about eighteen months), where they preached the gospel and strengthened Christians in their faith.

This region of Greece was steeped in religion. For example, the people of Athens wanted to ensure the favor of any deity they may have overlooked, so they dedicated an altar to "an unknown God" (Acts 17:23). Corinth itself housed a Temple of Apollo (see photo). A densely populated area, the city of Corinth probably had about eight hundred thousand residents during Paul's visit.

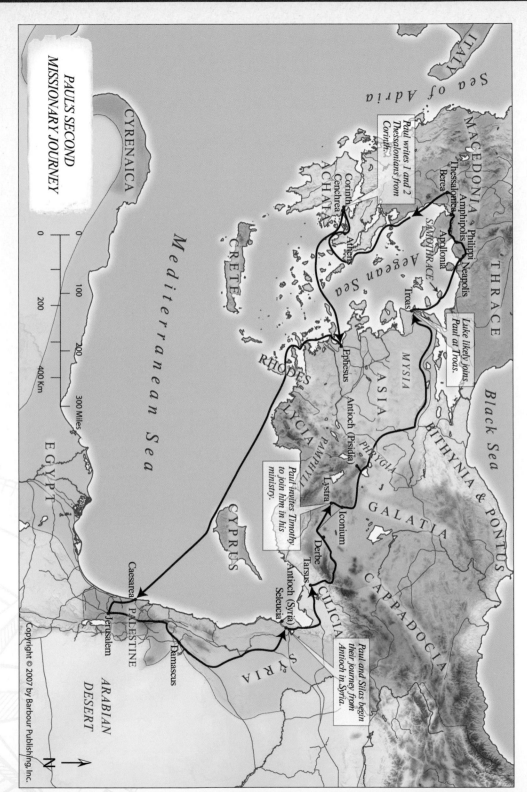

PAUL'S SECOND
MISSIONARY JOURNEY

ITALY

Sea of Adria

CYRENAICA

MACEDONIA

THRACE

Paul writes 1 and 2
Thessalonians from
Corinth.

Amphipolis
Thessalonica
Berea
Apollonia
Philippi
Neapolis
SAMOTHRACE

ACHAIA
Corinth
Cenchrea
Athens

Aegean Sea

Black Sea

Troas

Luke likely joins
Paul at Troas.

CRETE

Mediterranean Sea

MYSIA

ASIA

BITHYNIA & PONTUS

RHODES

Ephesus

Antioch (Pisidia)

PHRYGIA

LYCIA

PAMPHYLIA

Lystra

Iconium

GALATIA

CAPPADOCIA

Paul invites Timothy
to join him in his
ministry.

CYPRUS

Derbe

Antioch (Syria)
Seleucia

Tarsus

CILICIA

SYRIA

Paul and Silas begin
their journey from
Antioch in Syria.

Caesarea

PALESTINE

Jerusalem

Damascus

EGYPT

ARABIAN
DESERT

0   100   200   300 Miles

0   100   200   300   400 Km

N

Copyright © 2007 by Barbour Publishing, Inc.

157

PAUL'S THIRD MISSIONARY JOURNEY

Paul's third missionary journey began nearly as soon as his second journey ended. This journey, which occurred between AD 52 or 53 and AD 56 or 57, is recorded in Acts 18–21. Beginning in Antioch, this trip allowed Paul to retrace his steps to regions and cities he had already visited in order to preach the gospel to new listeners and bolster the faith of those already converted. The trip ended in Jerusalem with his arrest and Roman imprisonment.

Paul's longest stop during this trip was in the city of Ephesus, where he spent three years. There Paul met Apollos, spent time teaching him, and then sent him to minister to the church in Corinth.

Ephesus was a very advanced city in its day. Spiritually, the city was famous for its temple of Artemis—now known as one of the seven wonders of the world. As a place of worship, this ancient temple was four times the size of the Parthenon of Athens. Culturally, they could boast of sophisticated technology, such as a public latrine system (see photo). They built the latrine over a channel of moving water, which moved the waste out of the city. Socially, the culture encouraged indulgence in sexual promiscuity—with at least one large brothel that ran a successful business.

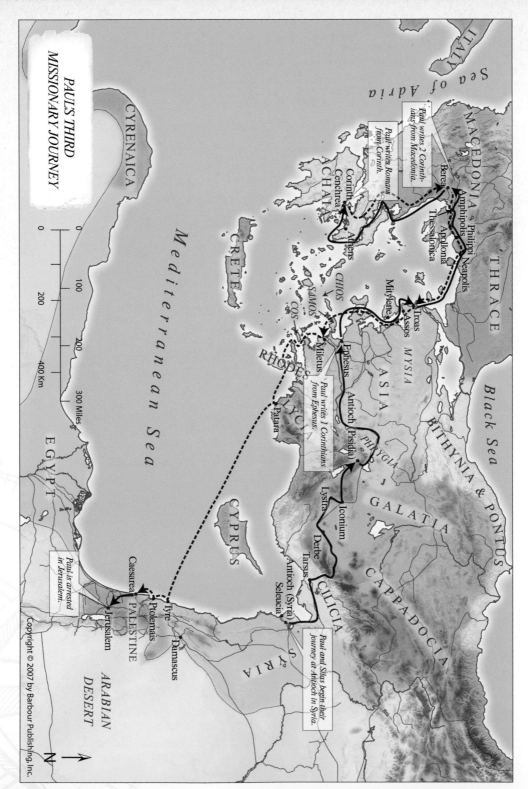

PAUL'S THIRD
MISSIONARY JOURNEY

Paul writes 2 Corinth-
ians from Macedonia.

Paul writes Romans
from Corinth.

Paul writes 1 Corinthians
from Ephesus.

Paul is arrested
in Jerusalem.

Paul and Silas begin their
journey at Antioch in Syria.

CYRENAICA

Sea of Adria

ITALY

MACEDONIA

THRACE

Philippi Neapolis
Amphipolis
Apollonia
Thessalonica
Berea

ACHAIA
Corinth
Cenchrea
Athens

CRETE

CHIOS

SAMOS

COS

RHODES

LYCIA
Patara

Mitylene
Troas
Assos

MYSIA

ASIA

Ephesus
Miletus

Antioch (Pisidia)

PHRYGIA

GALATIA

BITHYNIA & PONTUS

Black Sea

CAPPADOCIA

Lystra
Iconium

Derbe

Tarsus

Antioch (Syria)
Seleucia

CILICIA

SYRIA

Damascus

Mediterranean Sea

CYPRUS

EGYPT

Caesarea

Ptolemais
Tyre

Jerusalem
PALESTINE

ARABIAN
DESERT

0   100   200   300 Miles

0   200   400 Km

N

Copyright © 2007 by Barbour Publishing, Inc.

159

PAUL'S VOYAGE TO ROME

Certain Jewish leaders went to great lengths to stir up trouble for Paul. As they had done with Jesus, they hoped to use political pressure on the Roman leaders to have Paul executed or put in a position where he could be ambushed and killed en route to his trial (Acts 25:3). Perhaps because of his knowledge of their tendencies and plans, Paul appealed his case to Caesar himself—as was his right as a Roman citizen: "If, however, I am guilty of doing anything deserving death, I do not refuse to die. But if the charges brought against me by these Jews are not true, no one has the right to hand me over to them. I appeal to Caesar!" (Acts 25:11).

So the authorities turned Paul over to a Roman guard for escort to Rome where he would face charges in the Emperor's court.

While sailing to Rome, the ship encountered strong winds and was eventually wrecked on the Island of Malta. (See photo of traditional location in what is now know as St. Paul's Bay.)

Once in Rome, Paul lived under house arrest and wrote letters to the churches he had visited many times during his missionary journeys.

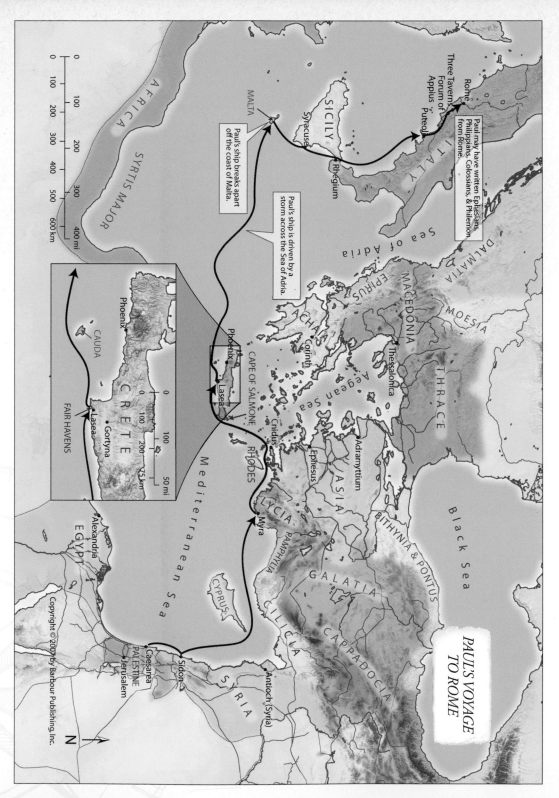

PAUL'S VOYAGE TO ROME

Paul may have written Ephesians, Philippians, Colossians, & Philemon from Rome.

Paul's ship breaks apart off the coast of Malta.

Paul's ship is driven by a storm across the Sea of Adria.

Three Taverns
Forum of Appius
Rome
Puteoli
Syracuse
Rhegium
SICILY
ITALY
DALMATIA
Sea of Adria

MALTA

SYRTIS MAJOR
AFRICA

Phoenix
CAUDA
CRETE
Gortyna
Lasea
FAIR HAVENS
Lasea
Phoenix
CAPE OF SALMONE

Corinth
ACHAIA
EPIRUS
MACEDONIA
Thessalonica
MOESIA
THRACE
Aegean Sea
Adramyttium
Ephesus
ASIA
BITHYNIA & PONTUS
Black Sea

Cnidus
RHODES
LYCIA
Myra
PAMPHYLIA
CILICIA
GALATIA
CAPPADOCIA

Mediterranean Sea
CYPRUS

Alexandria
EGYPT

Caesarea
Sidon
PALESTINE
Jerusalem
Antioch (Syria)
SYRIA

0 100 200 300 400 500 600 km
0 100 200 300 400 mi

0 100 200
0 25 50 mi
0 100 75 km

Copyright © 2007 by Barbour Publishing, Inc.

N

THE ROMAN EMPIRE IN THE TIME OF PAUL

At the peak of its expansion, Rome controlled 2.3 million square miles of land that encompassed the Mediterranean Sea. To a certain degree, Rome brought peace to its world and built many structures that still exist today (see photo of Roman Colosseum). And while the conquered people—especially the Jewish people in Palestine—resented Roman occupation, Paul and the early Christians benefited from the empire in the following ways:

- Initial Roman tolerance for Christianity trumped the Jewish leaders' persecution. For example, when the Jewish leaders wanted to put Paul to death, Rome's laws allowed Paul an appeal to Caesar. Once in Rome, Paul preached the gospel, helped establish the local church, and wrote letters that became part of the New Testament.

- Roman infrastructure also aided early Christians. The Roman roads and civil institutions allowed Christians to travel the Roman world quickly and without hindrance.

- The Roman peace (or Pax Romana) that occurred between 27 BC and AD 180 meant that the empire was not usually at war. Christians traveled freely by land and sea without major hindrances. The dense populations of many cities provided a large audience for the Christian message.

- A common language also united the western world. While many people groups held on to their local languages, Koine Greek became a universally understood language. The New Testament books were distributed in a common language, allowing a quick dissemination of the apostle's teaching.

- While the Roman government eventually turned hostile toward Christians—from the time of Nero (AD 54) until Constantine (AD 313)—the early decades of peace allowed orthodox Christianity to spread with little hindrance.

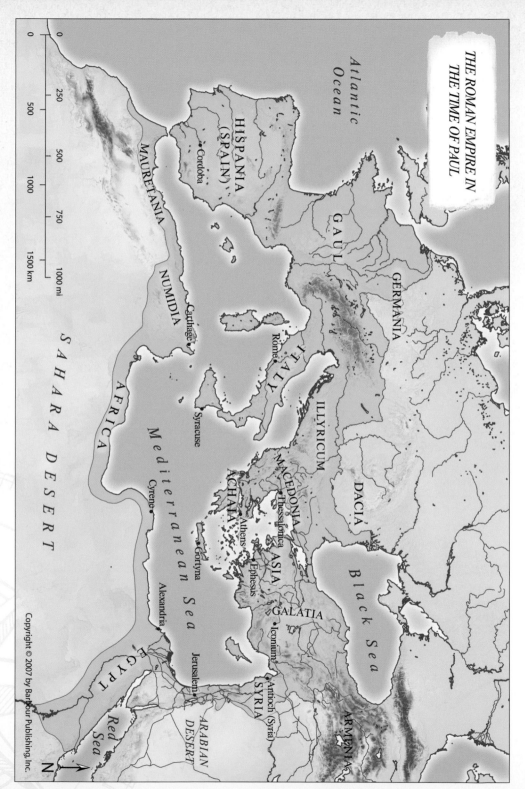

THE ROMAN EMPIRE IN
THE TIME OF PAUL

Atlantic
Ocean

HISPANIA
(SPAIN)

Córdoba

GAUL

GERMANIA

MAURETANIA

NUMIDIA

Carthage

SAHARA DESERT

AFRICA

Rome

ITALY

ILLYRICUM

DACIA

Syracuse

Mediterranean Sea

MACEDONIA

Thessalonica

ACHAIA

ASIA

Cyrene

Athens

Ephesus

GALATIA

Black Sea

Gortyna

Iconium

Alexandria

EGYPT

Jerusalem

Antioch (Syria)

SYRIA

ARMENIA

Red
Sea

ARABIAN
DESERT

0

250

500

1000

1500 km

0

250

500

750

1000 mi

N

THE CHURCHES OF REVELATION

Because of their dense population and key location along Roman routes, the seven cities mentioned in the book of Revelation became strategic during the spread of Christianity. While several of these cities were likely visited by Paul or other disciples, the apostle John wrote to them in order to wake them from the complacency they had fallen into. Below are the seven churches he mentions.

City	Reference	What We Know about Them
Ephesus	Rev. 2:1–7	John corrected them for leaving their first love. See more detailed description on page 158.
Smyrna	Rev. 2:8–11	This church suffered persecution and poverty. This city was known for its commerce and strategic harbors.
Pergamum	Rev. 2:12–17	This city played a vital role in Roman commerce and travel. A very worldly city, John reprimanded them for mixing accepted cultural practices into the doctrines of the church.
Thyatira	Rev. 2:18–29	This church was lured away from the gospel message by a prophetess reminiscent of the evil Jezebel.
Sardis	Rev. 3:1–6	The church in this city had been lulled to sleep by worldly influences. This city, known for its hedonistic temples and bath houses, seemed to have tempted the Christians away from their devotion for Christ.
Philadelphia	Rev. 3:7–13	John commended this church for waiting patiently for Jesus' return. Philadephia was a very religious city that contained many temples and places of worship.
Laodicea	Rev. 3:14–22	Laodicea was located near hot and cold springs, which would have made John's rebuke for being "lukewarm" very personal.

John wrote this letter while exiled on the island of Patmos (see photo). According to church tradition, John lived out his final years on this island. And while he had become elderly, tradition says that John was released in AD 96 upon the death of Emperor Domitian and the accession of the Emperor Nerva.

THE CHURCHES
OF REVELATION

✚ one of the seven
churches addressed
in Revelation

THRACE

Byzantium
Chalcedon
Nicomedia

Sea of Marmara

Sangarius River

Nicea

BITHYNIA

Cyzicus

0   50 mi
0   50 km

Abydos

Ilium (Troy)

Troas

Assos

Adramyttium

M Y S I A

Tembrus River

LESBOS
Mytilene

Pergamum

Selinus River

Thyatira

A S I A

CHIOS

Hermus River
Sardis
Philadelphia

Smyrna   *L Y D I A*

Apamea

Cayster River

Hierapolis

Ephesus
Magnesia   Tralles   Meander River   Laodicea
Colosse   ← Lycus
River

SAMOS
Priene

IKARIA
Miletus

C A R I A

PATMOS →

Halicarnassus

Indus River

L Y C I A

COS
Chnidus

Xanthus River

John is exiled to the island of Patmos,
where he writes the book of Revelation.

Rhodes

R H O D E S

Xanthus   Myra
Patara

N

Copyright © 2007 by Barbour Publishing, Inc.

ADDITIONAL INFORMATION:
ENEMIES OF ISRAEL

The people of Israel have had many enemies throughout their history. Here are some of the hostile neighbors we read about throughout biblical history.

Amalekites—These people were descendants of Esau and lived on the southern border of Israel near the desert region of Paran. They battled the people of Israel from the time of Moses (Exodus 17), through the time of the judges (Judges 6). King Saul and King David ultimately vanquished them (1 Samuel 15, 27, 30; 2 Samuel 8).

Ammonites—The people of Ammon were descendants of Abraham's nephew Lot. As relatives of God's people, God had instructed the people of Israel not to harm them during their conquest of Canaan (Deuteronomy 2:19). And since these people lived east of the Jordan River, they were left mostly undisturbed. During the time of the judges, however, the Ammonites raided Israel. Jephthah became a judge and defeated the Ammonites (Judges 11).

Amorites—The Amorites lived to the south of Israel and worshiped Baal and Asherah, which were common gods in the region. Saul defeated the Amorites in 2 Samuel 21:2.

Assyrians—The ten tribes of the Northern Kingdom were conquered and removed from the land by Assyria (2 Kings 17), which ruled much of the region between 934 and 612 BC. Assyria was known for being the cruelest and most vicious empire in the ancient world, inventing creative, painful ways to kill those who rebelled against them.

Babylonians—In the mid-600s BC, Babylon rose to power by defeating the Assyrians. Babylon's King Nebuchadnezzar defeated the southern kingdom of Israel (2 Chronicles 36) and took Daniel captive (Daniel 1). While in captivity, Daniel became a high-ranking advisor to the king of Babylon and later to the Medes and Persians who conquered the Babylonians (Daniel 6:28).

Canaanites—The term Canaanites referred to different tribes and peoples living in the land of Canaan during the time of Joshua (Joshua 3, 7, 9, 17). Generally, the people of the land worshiped Baal and Asherah. When Israel didn't conquer and remove these people completely as God had commanded, their influence in the areas of religion and culture began to have a negative influence on the spiritual life of God's people.

Edomites—These descendants of Esau lived to the southeast of Israel and on the opposite side of the Dead Sea. While Moses was leading the people to the promised land, the king of Edom refused to allow the Hebrews to pass through their land (Numbers 20). King David severely defeated the Edomites so that they never again became a serious threat to the people (2 Samuel 8). Edom existed in a vassal relationship with the Southern Kingdom for many years, occasionally securing independence.

Egyptians—Once Israel received its independence from Pharaoh, the people migrated and settled in the land of Israel. At times the nations of Israel and Egypt lived peacefully together. At other times, hostilities arose—most notably when Pharaoh Neco brought his army through the region (2 Kings 23; 2 Chronicles 35).

Greeks—The era of Israel's Northern and Southern Kingdoms was over by the time Greece rose to power (as prophesied in Daniel 8 and 10). The people of the Southern Kingdom were already subject to the Medes when Alexander the Great's army swept through the region. It was because of the Greek influence that people in the Mediterranean region spoke and wrote in Greek during the time of the early church.

Hittites—These people lived to the north of Israel in the region of Syria.

Moabites—Genesis 19 tells the story of Lot, Abraham's nephew, who had an incestuous relationship with his daughter. The resulting son, Moab, became the father of these people who lived east of the Jordan. A constant enemy of Israel, the Moabites joined forces with the Ammonites during the time of the judges (Judges 3). Later, the people of Moab fought a number of battles against the Northern and Southern Kingdoms (2 Kings 1, 3; 2 Chronicles 20).

Medes and Persians—These people lived in the region known as modern day Iran. While originally two distinct people groups, the Medes dominated the Persians and together they defeated the Babylonians, Assyrians, and the Jewish people under the Mede leadership of King Darius (Daniel 5:31). Eventually, however, the Persians usurped the Medes and retained the throne. It was under the reign of the Persians that the Bible records events that occurred under King Cyrus (2 Chronicles 36; Ezra 1). Later, the Persian king Xerxes chose Esther to be his queen (Esther 1). The Persians were ultimately conquered by Alexander the Great of Greece.

Philistines—The Philistines were known as seafaring people that had migrated from islands in the west. Once they settled in the southwestern portion of the land of Israel, they established a number of cities including Ashdod, Ashkelon, Ekron, Gath, and Gaza. The Philistines fought famous battles during the time of the judges, Saul, and David (Judges 13; 1 Samuel–2 Chronicles).

KEY CITIES IN ISRAEL

Below is a list of key biblical cities and some of the events that occurred in those cities. Because the history of biblical Israel lasted over a thousand years, the atmosphere, culture, and personality (and sometimes even the exact location) of the cities changed significantly during that time.

Beersheba—This city, along the southern end of Israel, was an important sanctuary for the people living near the Negev. Because this strategic city was in the southern region, it was often referred to as Israel's southern border. The Bible often refers to the land of Israel as stretching "from Dan to Beersheba" (2 Samuel 3:10). It was also the place where Abraham camped, dug a well, and banished Hagar and Ishmael (Genesis 21).

Bethel—The first significant biblical event that occurred in Bethel was when God appeared to Jacob (Genesis 35). When Israel divided into two kingdoms, Bethel was toward the southern end of the Northern Kingdom. King Jeroboam used this strategic location to build one of two high places for worship—the other was built in Dan (1 Kings 12).

Bethany—This city was important during Jesus' ministry. It was the home of Mary, Martha, and Lazarus— and the location Jesus raised Lazarus from the dead (John 11). It was the city where Jesus spent most of His final week as well as the location of His ascension into heaven (Luke 24).

Bethlehem—While known as the birthplace of Jesus (Luke 2), this was also the city where Ruth and Boaz met and were married (Ruth 2, 4). It also was the birthplace of King David (1 Samuel 16).

Cana—While the exact location of Cana is uncertain, the town was certainly located near Nazareth where Jesus and His mother lived. When they were invited to a wedding at Cana, Jesus and Mary attended the event where Jesus performed His first miracle (John 2).

Capernaum—This city became one of the centers of Jesus' teaching ministry. A practical choice, it was the hometown of about half of Jesus' disciples and was located on some strategic trade routes—allowing a great number of people exposure to Jesus and His teaching.

Dan—This city was at the northernmost end of Israel and served as a convenient border and point of reference, just as Beersheba did in the south. When the Northern Kingdom became independent by rebelling against the line of David, King Jeroboam created a worship center in an effort to deter his citizens from journeying to Jerusalem to worship (1 Kings 12).

Dothan—When Jacob sent his son Joseph to check on his other brothers, Joseph went to Dothan where he was sold into slavery (Genesis 37). Centuries later, the army of Aram surrounded the city in a futile effort to capture Elisha (2 Kings 6).

En Gedi—David hid from King Saul at En Gedi. Once while David was hiding in a cave, King Saul unknowingly entered the same cave to relieve himself. David cut off part of Saul's robe but left the king unharmed to prove that he had no intention of killing him though he had an easy opportunity (1 Samuel 24).

Gilead—East of the Jordan River there is a twenty-mile strip of lush land well-suited for grazing animals. In addition to pasturelands, parts of the region are also heavily forested. This is a location where many people in the Bible found refuge, including Jacob and David. It was also in this forest that Absalom's hair became tangled in a tree before he was killed (2 Samuel 17–18).

Hebron—Hebron became Abraham's home after he parted ways with his nephew, Lot, as recorded in Genesis 13. Also located here is the traditional site of Abraham's tomb (Genesis 23). It was here that King David established his first capital city before relocating it to Jerusalem (2 Samuel 2).

Jericho—The city of Jericho is best known for the battle that occurred when the Israelites marched around the city for seven days before the walls crashed down (Joshua 6). Centuries later, the city was rebuilt and history tells us that the city became the winter home of King Herod. Other well-known Bible characters had a home here, including blind Bartimaeus and Zacchaeus (Mark 10; Luke 19).

Jerusalem—The "city of David" had a long history and was occupied for at least two thousand years before David conquered it and made it his capital. Throughout the history of the Southern Kingdom, Jerusalem was the political and spiritual center of Israelite life and hosted the temple and the kings' palaces. The city has been destroyed and rebuilt many times over the years. At the time of Jesus, the city was home to a new temple built by Herod. Jerusalem was also the location of Jesus' crucifixion.

Joppa—The prophet Jonah started his trip from Joppa when running from God's instruction (Jonah 1:3). This was also the city where Peter raised Tabitha from the dead and had a vision instructing him to eat non-kosher food (Acts 9–11).

Nazareth—This small and insignificant community was the boyhood home of Jesus. Its obscurity helps explain Nathanael's bewilderment when he learned Jesus' hometown: "Can anything good come from there?" (John 1:46).

Samaria—In Jesus' day, the word Samaria referred to a region where many people of mixed ethnic descent lived. (Jesus used this fact to illustrate the kindness of the Good Samaritan in Luke 10.) Before Jesus' day, however, Samaria referred to a city that was forty miles north of Jerusalem. King Omri of the Northern Kingdom established the city and made it his capital (1 Kings 16).

Shechem—Shechem was the site of many important events in the history of the people of Israel. It was here that God appeared to Abraham and promised to give him the land of Canaan (Genesis 12:6–7). It was also the location where the people renewed their allegiance to God under Joshua (Joshua 24). Later, this city became a city of refuge and served as a capital city for the Northern Kingdom.

Tyre—Tyre was a city located fourteen miles north of the border of Israel, yet was an important city to King David and King Solomon. Without a strategic seaport within the borders of Israel, the kings of Israel fostered good relationships with the people of Tyre, which allowed them to move many goods through their seaport (1 Kings 5).

ADDITIONAL INFORMATION:
WATER IN ISRAEL

Since the terrain of Israel can change from lush green to harsh wilderness within a few miles, it is understandable why water became such an important image to the biblical writers. Since much of the land of Israel is in a dry region, the work of digging wells and cisterns became incredibly important, and this work is often referred to in the Old Testament narratives. The areas of dry climate also yielded many powerful, poetic images such as Psalm 42:1: "As the deer pants for streams of water, so my soul pants for you, O God."

While a portion of Israel maintains a dry climate, there are also areas of the country that are quite wet and green. Below are some of the key bodies of water located within the boundaries of Israel.

The Sea of Galilee is fourteen miles long, yet only three to four miles wide. Located in the northern portion of the land, this lake had many towns surrounding it. This freshwater lake provided necessary water for the region as well as fish for food. Many of Jesus' disciples were fishermen and would have carried out their trade on this lake. In the Old Testament, this body of water was called the Sea of Kinnereth (Numbers 34:10; Joshua 13:27). Today, it is referred to as Lake Tiberias or Lake Kinneret.

The Jordan River is a 156-mile river that runs from the northern region near the Sea of Galilee and empties into the salty Dead Sea. This river runs in a generally southern direction and provides much of the land with fresh water. The Jordan River was the location of many miracles in the Bible, including miraculous crossings by Joshua, Elijah, and Elisha (Joshua 3; 2 Kings 2). It was also the location where Naaman bathed and was cleansed of leprosy (2 Kings 5), and where Jesus was baptized by John the Baptist (Matthew 3). Today the Jordan River helps form borders between Israel and her neighbors. Its depth has been reduced because of irrigation projects completed by the countries of Israel and Jordan.

The Dead Sea is a lake in the southern half of Israel's territory. The Dead Sea is forty-two miles long and at its greatest breadth eleven miles wide. This salt lake is nearly nine

times saltier than the ocean. The only tributary into the Dead Sea is the Jordan River, and there are no streams or water outlets that lead out of the Dead Sea. In addition, the region itself only receives two to four inches of rain per year. While the Dead Sea served as a useful border between the lands of Israel, Moab, and Edom, it is said that Solomon, Aristotle, Herod, and the Queen of Sheba all enjoyed using the mineral-rich waters from the Dead Sea for medicinal purposes. The picture on this page is from the shores of this salt sea.

The Mediterranean Sea (also called "The Great Sea" or "The Sea") borders Israel, much of southern Europe, and northern Africa. This body of water helped connect Israel to the rest of the known world. Solomon used it to float timbers of cedar from Lebanon for his building projects near Jerusalem as well as to expand Israel's economy (1 Kings 5). Paul traveled it extensively, bringing the message of Christianity to many of the cities that bordered the Sea.

ADDITIONAL INFORMATION:
JEWISH CALENDAR

The traditional Hebrew calendar mentioned in the Bible uses different months than we are used to in our Western culture, which follows the Gregorian calendar system. In most of the Bible, the months are referred to by their number (for example, "in the fourth month"). When the Jewish people returned from exile, however, they began to call months by specific Babylonian names. And while the first month of the Jewish year is Nisan, the Jewish New Year is actually celebrated in the seventh month. That may seem unusual to our modern system—but we have our own similar anomalies (such as starting a new school year in September). Below is a list of Jewish months with their Gregorian equivalents.

MONTH	HEBREW MONTH	WHEN IT OCCURS IN THE GREGORIAN CALENDAR
1st month	Nisan	March–April
2nd month	Iyar	April–May
3rd month	Sivan	May–June
4th month	Tammuz	June–July
5th month	Ab	July–August
6th month	Elul	August–September
7th month	Tishri	September–October
8th month	Heshvan	October–November
9th month	Chislev	November–December
10th month	Tebeth	December–January
11th month	Shebat	January–February
12th month	Adar	February–March

ADDITIONAL INFORMATION:
TABLE OF WEIGHTS AND MEASURES

BIBLE	AMERICAN/ BRITISH	METRIC
MEASURES OF LENGTH		
cubit	1.5 feet	0.46 meter
span	9 inches	22.9 centimeters
handbreadth	3 inches	7.6 centimeters
reed (or measuring rod or fathom)	9 feet	2.7 meters
a sabbath's day journey	0.5 mile	0.8 kilometer
a day's journey	24 miles	38.6 kilometers
MEASURES OF WEIGHT (CURRENCY)		
talent	75 pounds	34 kilograms
mina	1.2 pounds	0.5 kilogram
shekel	0.4 ounce	10.2 grams
drachma	0.3 ounce	7.7 grams
bekah	0.2 ounce	5.2 grams
gerah	0.02 ounce	0.6 gram
MEASURES OF DRY GOODS		
cor (or homer)	6.2 bushels	220 liters
ephah	0.5 bushels	18.2 liters
seah	6.4 quarts	6.1 liters
omer	1.9 quarts	1.8 liters
MEASURES OF LIQUID GOODS		
bath	5.8 gallons	21.9 liters
hin	1 gallon	3.8 liters
log	0.3 quart	0.3 liter

To find the value of money in terms of today's currency, multiply the money's weight against the current values of gold and silver. For example, to find the value of a silver shekel, multiply 0.4 ounces against the today's trading rate of silver.

While this table provides good estimates, biblical scholars often differ on the exact figures of each measurement.

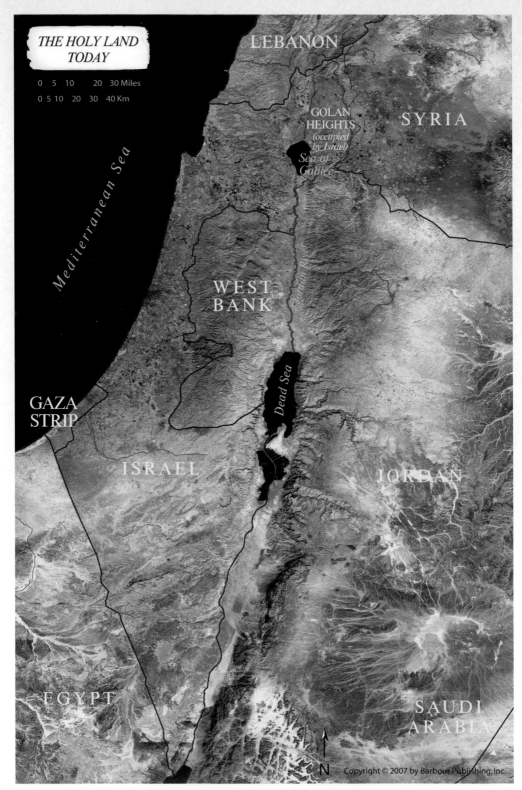

Satellite photo of the Holy Land today.

ABOUT THE CONTRIBUTORS

David Barrett is a full-time web developer. His love for the Bible and his training in editing, ancient languages, and computer programming have cultivated a lasting fascination with Bible geography and the illumination it brings to scripture. Along with professional Bible maps and resources, David has developed Bible Mapper software (www. biblemapper.com), a tool that enables users to create very accurate, customized maps of Bible lands or research a particular aspect of Bible history and geography. David lives in Chambersburg, Pennsylvania, with his wife, Anisea, and their five children.

Todd Bolen is Professor of Biblical Studies at The Master's University in Santa Clarita, California. For many years, Dr. Bolen taught at TMU's Israel Bible Extension campus, leading geography field trips and participating in archaeological excavations. He has written articles for the *Archaeological Study Bible*, authored the notes for 2 Kings for the *NIV Biblical Theology Study Bible*, and contributed essays to the *Lexham Geographic Commentary* series. Dr. Bolen is the founder of BiblePlaces.com and the creator of the *Pictorial Library of Bible Lands* and the *Photo Companion to the Bible*.

Christopher D. Hudson is the president of Peachtree Publishing Services. Peachtree's mission is to protect and advance God's Word by proofreading Bibles and developing resources that help readers engage the Bible. Christopher is the editor of Barbour Publishing's *KJV Study Bible* and the author of *100 Names of God* (Rose) and *The Most Significant Teachings in the Bible* (Zondervan). Christopher and his wife of nearly thirty years serve their local church in Northern Illinois and enjoy traveling to visit their three adult children.